EUROPE IN MAPS

EUROPE IN MAPS

Contents of Book 2

1. Finse. Part of the Norwegian high fjell.
2. Røros. An old mining township in eastern Norway.
3. Karlstad. A centre of the Swedish timber industry.
4. Vällingby. A new town in Greater Stockholm.
5. Sönder Vissing. A dairy farming district in East Jutland.
6. The North East Polder. Reclamation and Colonisation of a new polder area.
7. Nieuw Schoonebeek. Economic change along the Dutch-German border.
8. Beauce, Brie, Champagne and Normandy. Agricultural Contrasts in the Paris Basin.
9. Hagondange. An iron and steel works in the Moselle Valley.
10. Sète. A section of the Bas Languedoc coast.
11. Ostend. A North Sea packet station.
12. Meerfeld and Daun. A volcanic landscape of the Rhine Highlands.
13. Gross Ilsede. A section of the West German Börde.
14. Speyer. An historic town of the Rhine Rift valley.
15. Zürich. A commercial and industrial centre on the Swiss Plateau.
16. La Chaux de Fonds. A Jura landscape.

EUROPE IN MAPS
Topographical Map Studies of Western Europe

BOOK ONE

R. Knowles
Lecturer in Geography
North-Western Polytechnic, London

P. W. E. Stowe
Headmaster
Riversmead School, Cheshunt

Longman

Contents	Page
The Regional Setting of the Study Areas	8
Keys to Norwegian, Swedish, Danish, Dutch and Belgian Maps	10
West European Topographical Maps	12
1 Aurland. A Fjord Coast	14
2 Svolvær. A Lofoten Fishing Town	18
3 Kiruna. An Arctic Mining Settlement	22
4 Copenhagen	26
5 Geestmerambacht. A Polder Landscape	30
6 Liège. An Old Industrial Landscape	36
7 Duisburg. A Section of the Ruhr Conurbation	42
8 Reutlingen. Part of the South German Scarplands	48
9 Kaub. A Section of the Rhine Gorge	54
10 Plön. A Landscape of Young Glacial Deposits	58
11 Wolfsburg. An Area of Recent Industrialisation	62
12 Rouen. A Bridge Point Settlement	66
13 Carcassonne. An Historic Town of the Midi	70
14 Solliès Pont. A Provençal Landscape	74
15 Marseilles and the Etang de Berre. A Study in Port Growth	78
16 The Engadine. An Alpine Valley	86
17 The Gorner Glacier	90
Keys to West German, French and Swiss Maps	94
Linear Scales and Conversion Tables	96

Maps	Page
1 Aurland, Norway 1:50,000	14
2 Svolvær, Norway 1:100,000	18
3 Kiruna, Sweden 1:100,000	22
4 Copenhagen, Denmark 1:100,000	26
5 Geestmerambacht Polder, Netherlands 1:50,000	30
6 Broek op Langedijk, Netherlands 1:25,000	34
7 Liège, Belgium 1:50,000	38
8 Duisburg-Ruhrort, West Germany 1:50,000	42
9 Reutlingen, West Germany 1:50,000	50
10 Kaub, West Germany 1:50,000	54
11 Plön, West Germany 1:50,000	58
12 Wolfsburg, West Germany 1:50,000	62
13 Rouen, France 1:50,000	66
14 Carcassonne, France 1:25,000	70
15 Solliès-Pont, France 1:50,000	74
16 Marseilles, France 1:50,000	78
17 Etang de Berre, France 1:50,000	82
18 Engadine, Switzerland 1:50,000	86
19 Gorner Glacier, Switzerland 1:50,000	90

LONGMAN GROUP LIMITED
London
*Associated companies, branches
and representatives
throughout the world*

© Longman Group Ltd 1969

All rights reserved. No part of this publication may be reproduced, stored in a retrieval system, or transmitted in any form, or by any means electronic, mechanical, photocopying, recording, or otherwise without the prior permission of the Copyright owner.

First published 1969
Fifth impression 1974

ISBN 0 582 31029 6

Printed in Hong Kong by The Continental Printing Co. Ltd.

	Photographs	Page
1	Aurlandsfjord	15
2	Svolvær, Lofoten	19
3	Kiruna and the Kirunavaara Iron working	23
4	Copenhagen	27
5	Geestmerambacht Polder	31
6	Broek op Langedijk	34
7	The Meuse Valley	39
8	The Docks at Duisburg-Ruhrort	43
9	The Rhine front at Duisburg	44
10	Reutlingen and Pfullingen	51
11	Pfullingen	53
12	The Rhine Gorge	55
13	Plön, Schleswig-Holstein	59
14	The Volkswagen Plant at Wolfsburg	63
15	The Seine at Rouen	67
16	Carcassonne	71
17	Solliès Pont, Plain of the Gapeau	74
18	Marseilles harbour	78
19	Lavéra Oil Refinery	83
20	The Engadine Valley	87
21	The Gorner Glacier and Breithorn	91
22	The Gorner Glacier and Monte Rosa	93

	Figures	Page
1	Structure of Europe and Location of Study Areas	9
2	Sogne Fjord	16
3	The Lofoten Islands	18
4	Sketch map of Kiruna	25
5	The growth of Copenhagen 1850–1950	28
6	North Holland	32
7	The coalfields of Belgium and neighbouring areas	36
8	Section across the Meuse valley	37
9	The Ruhr	44
10	Generalised section across the Ruhr coalfield	45
11	Duisburg: Industrial location	46
12	The Structure of South West Germany	48
13	Section across the South German Scarplands	49
14	The Rhine Highlands	56
15	Eastern Schleswig-Holstein	60
16	Part of the North German Plain	64
17	The Carcassonne Gap	72
18	Provence	75
19	Climate Graphs for Cuers, Provence	76
20	Land use around Solliès Pont	77
21	Position of Marseilles	79
22	The Growth Elements of Central Marseilles	80
23	Surface and Bedrock contours for the Gorner Glacier	92

Acknowledgements

We are pleased to acknowledge the many individuals and organisations who have helped in the preparation of this book, particularly by the provision of up-to-date statistical material and other information about the study areas. In particular we would like to thank Statistisk Sentralbyrå, Oslo; Per Mietle of Fiskeridirektøren, Bergen; Sven-Eric Brunnsjö, Director of Public Relations for L.K.A.B., Stockholm; The Royal Danish Embassy in London; The Royal Netherlands Embassy, London; The Dutch Ministry of Agriculture; G. Jackson; A. Dufrasne of the Institut National de Statistique Belgique; L. Van Malderen of the Ministère des Affairs Economiques (Administration des Mines); The Information Service of the European Community; The Niederrheinische Industrie und Handelskammer, Duisburg-Wesel; The Industrie und Handelskammer in Reutlingen; Dr. Brustmann of the Industrie und Handelskammer, Koblenz; A. D. Wheatley of Volkswagen Motors Ltd.; Niedersächsisches Landesverwaltungsamt Statistik; The Industrie und Handelskammer, Braunschweig; R. Broschart of the Economic Section of the Embassy of the Federal German Republic, London; M. Jackson; P. J. T. Morrill; The Institut National de la Statistique et des Etudes Economiques, Paris; The French Embassy, London; Joseph Sabiayrolles, President of the Syndicat d'Initiativ, Carcassonne and the Chambre de Commerce, Carcassonne; The Direction Départementale de l'Agriculture, Département du Var; The Institut de Recherches Economiques et Sociales, Marseilles; The Chambre de Commerce et d'Industrie, Marseilles; and Dr. G. Elliston of the Department of Geography in Hull University.

Photographs have been obtained from a variety of sources which are acknowledged in each case. Maps and diagrams have been especially drawn for the book by K. Wass, chief draughtsman in the Department of Geography, University College, London. Fig. 5 is reproduced from a map by Niels Nielsen in *Guide Book to Denmark* published by the Geographical Institute of Copenhagen University and fig. 11 is based on a map by the Industrie und Verkehrskarten Institut, Ivis-Verlag, Düsseldorf. In the case of maps which have been partly based on other sources the original map has been stated.

Among the numerous works used in the preparation of this book mention should be made of the particularly valuable help received from W. R. Mead's *Economic Geography Of The Scandinavian States And Finland, The Geography Of Norden* edited by A. Sømme, R. E. Dickinson's *Germany* and F. J. Monkhouse's *Western Europe*. Two papers were drawn on extensively for Studies 6 and 8; namely, *Liège And The Problems Of Southern Belgium* by T. H. Elkins and *The South German Scarplands In The Vicinity of Tübingen* by T. H. Elkins and E. M. Yates. Both papers were originally published in 'Geography'.

We are indebted to the following for permission to reproduce questions from past examination papers: Joint Matriculation Board for two questions; Oxford and Cambridge Schools Examination Board for fourteen questions (July 1962, 1963 and 1964 papers); Southern Universities Joint Board for School Examinations for one question (June 1963 paper); Welsh Joint Education Committee for four questions (July 1963, 1964 and 1966 papers). Finally, thanks are due to B. Barbour-Hill for typing the manuscript.

Foreword

This book has been written with the aim of providing a series of studies of small and distinctive areas in western Europe. The studies are based upon extracts from national topographical maps and aerial photographs. The commentaries are concerned with the information provided by the maps and photographs, but in many cases the limitations of these two sources are soon apparent and supplementary material has been introduced, especially on land use and industrial geography.

It is hoped that the book will be of value in two ways. Firstly, it should enable a student to become familiar with the cartographic styles of foreign maps and thus play a useful role in mapwork studies. Secondly, the use of such samples will be valuable in connection with regional work on western Europe. It has been found that detailed studies of small, specific areas can usefully precede, or alternatively substantiate, the generalisations that are common in many standard regional geographies. The book is therefore complementary to regional texts rather than alternative to them.

Inevitably the choice of study areas is a subjective one. The aim has been to cover as wide a range as possible of aspects of physical, agricultural, industrial and settlement geography. However, the non-availability of both up-to-date map sheets and good photographs has precluded studies of many interesting areas. This is especially true of France, where much of the west and central part of the country is mapped only on outdated series.

The book has been prepared particularly with the needs of 'A' level and first year university students in mind, and assumes a basic knowledge of physical and human geography. Although many of the questions are based entirely on an understanding of the map extracts, others have been included which will require reference to regional texts and an appreciation of the geography of other parts of western Europe. There is certainly much scope for further cartographical exercises, which may be devised to fit individual requirements. In many cases it would be valuable for students to have access to the full map sheets from which the extracts have been taken.

Finally, it should be emphasised that each district studied possesses its own individuality, a product of its landscape, its people and its history. Although parallels may be drawn with other areas, it would be unwise to think of these studies as 'type' areas representative of large tracts of western Europe. The differences are frequently of more significance than the similarities. The studies should rather be thought of as illustrating the interaction of various geographical factors in the evolution of a distinctive landscape; only in this sense are they applicable to other parts of western Europe from which the extracts have been taken.

R. KNOWLES   P. W. E. STOWE

The Regional Setting of the Study Areas

(Numbers in bold type refer to studies included in the book).

The series of seventeen studies presented in the book is an attempt to provide a cross section of the geography of western Europe from various standpoints. In terms of structure Europe may be divided into a number of distinct regions (fig. 1). Most of Norway belongs to Caledonian Europe, an area of Cambrian and Silurian rocks folded in late Silurian times and since subjected to changes of base level and long periods of denudation. The Alps, represented in this work by the studies of the Engadine (**16**) and the Gorner Glacier (**17**), belong to the youngest fold mountain zone of Europe, while many upland areas, including those bordering the Rhine Gorge (**9**), are a result of the Hercynian earth movements, intermediate in age between the former two. In this case remnants of an earlier planation are to be seen in the level surfaces of the Taunus and Hunsrück plateaux. Much of the physical, and indeed human, geography of Europe has been modified by the Quaternary glaciation. The work of glaciers at the present time can be seen in the Gorner area (**17**), while mountainous landscapes such as those of Aurlandsfjord (**1**), the Lofoten Islands (**2**) and the Engadine (**16**) show the results of their work in recent times. At the maximum extent of the Quaternary glaciation much of northern Europe was covered by great ice sheets. These left a bewildering variety of landscape features. The outwash sands and gravels of the geest country, products of fluvioglacial, rather than purely glacial, action, dominate the landscapes of much of northern Germany, as in the Wolfsburg district (**11**), but ground moraine features are to be found in eastern Denmark and eastern Schleswig-Holstein (**10**). While it is obviously impossible in a work of such limited size to deal with the whole range of landforms, nevertheless the various studies also provide examples of a variety of coastal and river features.

In a similar way a transect of the human geography of western Europe is provided. Although the use of a topographical map in this connection has its limitations, the variations in quality and type of agriculture are readily apparent. The difficult environments, both physically and climatically, of Aurlandsfjord (**1**) and the Engadine (**16**) impose a semi-subsistence form of agriculture upon their inhabitants, eked out by fishing, forestry or tourism. By contrast the farmer of the geestlands has, by his own efforts and subsidies from former governments bent on self-sufficiency, improved his podsolised soils to produce good crops of sugar-beet, potatoes and cereals. The more specialised farmers of Europe are also represented. On the polders of the Netherlands, where agriculture has become increasingly specialised, the producers of cereals, vegetables and dairy produce have made high standards of living for themselves, although even these regions are not without their problem areas, as the Geestmerambacht study (**5**) shows. The warm lands of Provence (**14**) provide another contrast in style of agriculture. Here man has made use of his one great asset, the climate, and provides fruit and wine for markets in the cooler north.

The industrial geography of western Europe can also be studied with success through the use of topographical maps, although their value is enhanced by additional statistical data and factory location maps. The contrasts here lie between the old and the new. The Ruhr (**7**) and the Sambre-Meuse valley (**6**), with their activity dating mainly from the 19th century, contrast with settings such as Wolfsburg (**11**) and the Etang de Berre (**15**), where industry has been established only during the last 30 years. There are also many instances of sites significant in the past for their craft industries. Thus both Reutlingen (**8**) and Rouen (**12**) have shown steady development from medieval times to the present day, a result of excellent positional, site and labour advantages. Europe is also important for its extractive industries, and the study of Kiruna (**3**) shows the difficulties under which men will work if the reward is great enough. No geography of western Europe would be complete without reference to its towns. Many of these date from pre-Roman times, and studies such as those of Rouen (**12**) and Carcassonne (**13**) emphasize the timeless advantages possessed by these settlements. From the selection of towns covered by these studies it is possible to see something of the different types which have evolved and the variations resulting from factors of site, planning ideas in favour during the periods of growth and changes in function. Thus, the medieval fortifications of Carcassonne (**13**) may be contrasted with the urban plan of Wolfsburg (**11**) which illustrates modern ideas. Towns such as those of Liège (**6**) and Duisburg (**7**) show the way in which 19th-century *laissez-faire* produced a random sprawl of building ill-adapted to the needs of today. The lifeblood of western Europe lies in its trade, and in this field the studies of Copenhagen (**4**), Rouen (**12**) and Marseilles (**15**) illustrate different types of ports and the conditions under which a great port may develop.

Further reading

HARRISON CHURCH, R. J., HALL, P., LAWRENCE, G. R. P., MEAD, W. R., MUTTON, A. *An Advanced Geography of Northern and Western Europe,* Hulton, 1967.
HOUSTON, J. M. *A Social Geography of Europe,* Duckworth, 1963.
MONKHOUSE, F. J. *The Countries of North-Western Europe,* Longmans, 1965.
OGILVIE, A. G. *Europe and its Borderlands,* Nelson, 1957.
POWRIE, P. J. and MANSFIELD, A. J. *North West Europe,* 2nd edn, Harrap, 1964.
SHACKLETON, M. R. *Europe,* 7th edn, Longmans, 1965.

EGLI, E. and MULLER, H. R. *Europe from the Air*, Harrap, 1959.
SMITH, C. T. *An Historical Geography of Western Europe Before 1800*, Longmans, 1967.
SCARGILL, D. I. *Economic Geography of France*, Macmillan, 1968.
DOLLFUS, J. *France: Its Geography and Growth*, John Murray, 1969.

Exercises

1. In what ways has glacial deposition affected the agriculture of western Europe excluding Britain? (O. & C.)
2. Assess the effects of glaciation on the human geography of one of the following: Norway, Scotland, Sweden or Switzerland. (London.)
3. Relate the natural vegetation of Europe to the dominant physical controls. (J.M.B.)
4. With reference to a selection of the study areas, examine the extent to which landscapes in western Europe are determined by structural factors.
5. Discuss the relative importance of physical and human factors in the agricultural geography of Mediterranean France. (W.J.E.C.)
6. With reference to western Europe, examine the conditions under which farming becomes highly specialised.
7. How far does the study of a land use map enable one to understand the farming of an area?
8. Examine the geographical basis of one major area of steel production within north-western Europe. (London.)
9. By reference to specific examples, discuss the factors which favour the growth of heavy chemical industries. (O. & C.)
10. Discuss the assertion that successful industrialisation requires more than the presence of raw materials. (O. & C.)
11. Why are certain of the areas of 'old' industry in western Europe still flourishing and important while others appear to face a future of difficulty and decline?
12. Examine the factors which are producing changes in the pattern of industrial location in western Europe.
13. Describe the specific problems associated with mining either in areas of highly folded and faulted rocks or in high latitudes. (O. & C.)
14. 'The genesis and development of towns have very often been due to some obstacle where man has had to halt and change his means of transport.' Amplify and give examples. (O. & C.)
15. Illustrate the statement that the type of rural settlement reflects both land use and history. (O. & C.)
16. With reference to two ports in western Europe, show how the present pattern of industry has been affected by their history.
17. Show how large towns tend to affect the non-industrial land use of surrounding areas. (O. & C.)
18. Show how the growth of towns is both encouraged and limited by geographical conditions. (O. & C.)
19. Why do some canals in Europe remain important means of transport at the present time? (O. & C.)
20. Assess the role of the topographical map in geographical study. (O. & C.)
21. Compare the sites, situations and functions of one seaport and one inland river port in north-western Europe. (London.)
22. Compare the geography of any two major sea ports in north-western Europe. (London.)

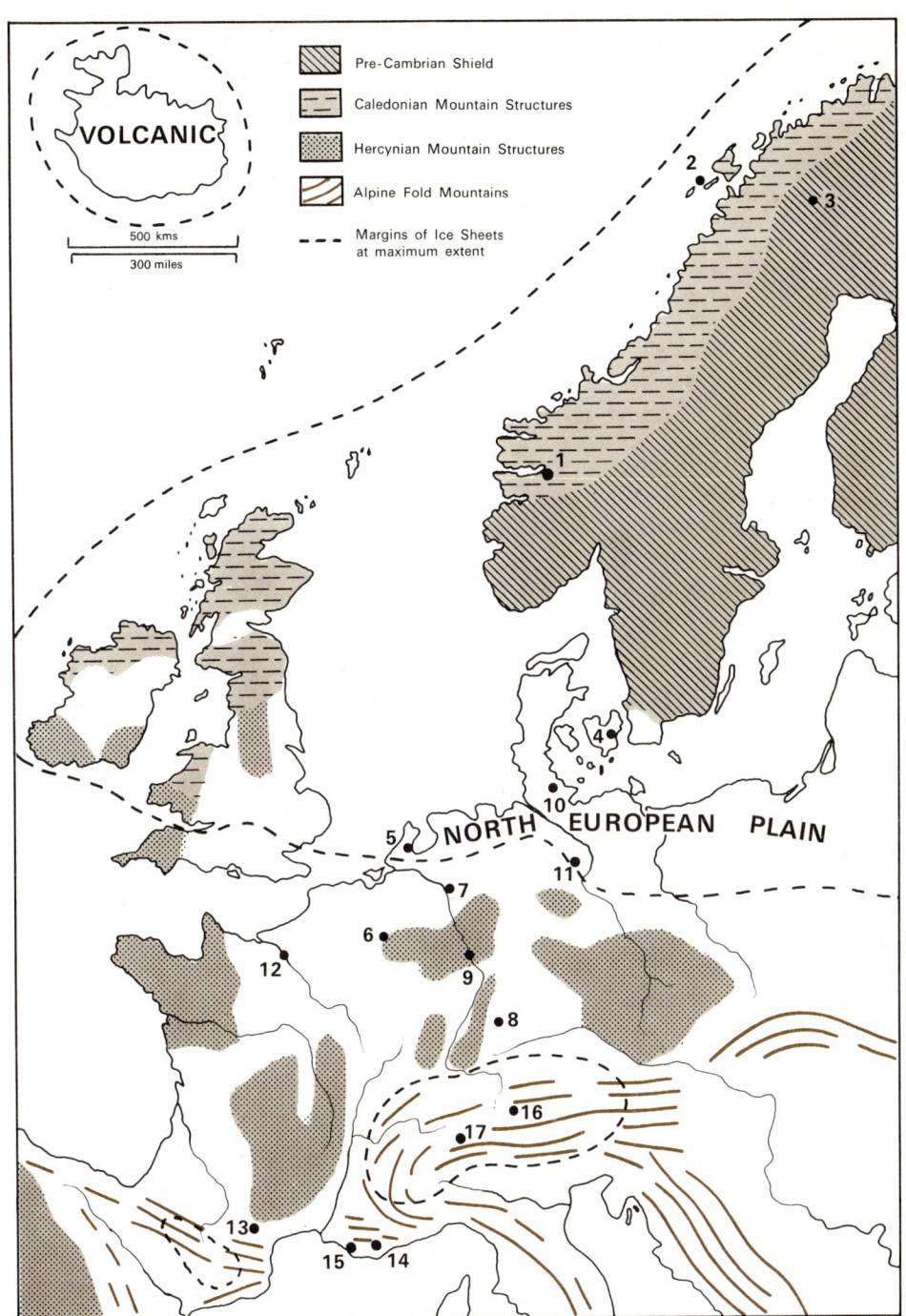

Figure 1. Structural map of Europe and location of study areas.

1 Aurlandsfjord
2 Svolvær, Lofoten
3 Kiruna
4 Copenhagen
5 Geestmerambacht
6 Liège
7 Duisburg
8 Reutlingen
9 Kaub
10 Plön
11 Wolfsburg
12 Rouen
13 Carcassonne
14 Solliès-Pont
15 Marseilles
16 Engadine
17 Gorner Glacier

Key Symbols Norwegian 1:50 000 Map Series

Only those symbols necessary for interpretation of the map extracts have been listed. These are not comprehensive lists of symbols.

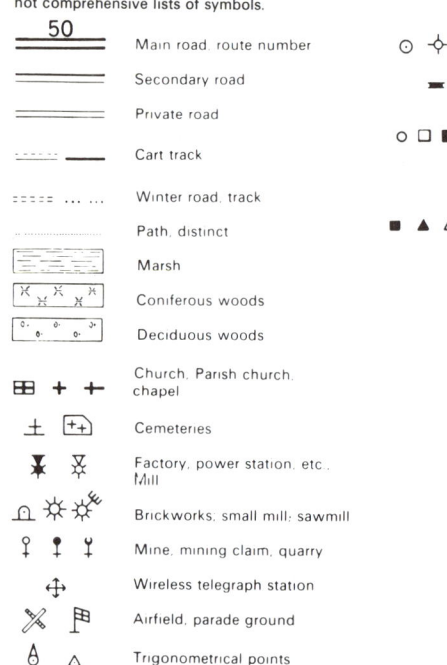

50	Main road, route number
	Secondary road
	Private road
	Cart track
	Winter road, track
	Path, distinct
	Marsh
	Coniferous woods
	Deciduous woods
	Church, Parish church, chapel
	Cemeteries
	Factory, power station, etc., Mill
	Brickworks, small mill; sawmill
	Mine, mining claim, quarry
	Wireless telegraph station
	Airfield, parade ground
	Trigonometrical points
⊙ ✦ ☀	Lighthouse, light; beacon; air navigation light
	Fishers or hunters cabin, cattle camp, etc.
○ □ ■ ●	Farms: farm, mountain pasture
■ ▲ ♦	Cottage, school, hotel, meeting house, tourist shelter, inn, sports-hunters cabin, small farm, small power station, mill, etc.

1:100 000 Map Series

	Church
o	Farm
•	Smallholding, saeter
▪	House, school, meeting house, club-house, small business property, etc.
▪	Hotel, tourist hut, boarding house
–	Fishing hut, shooting lodge
✱	Factory, big business property, power station, mill, etc.
⚬	Trigonometrical point
⊙	Lighthouse, beacon
✧	Buoy
+	Rock above water
+	Rock below water
----	Rural and urban district boundaries
	Main road
	Local road
	Private road
	Cart track
	Farm track
	Path
	Marked path
	Poorly marked path
	Telephone, telegraph line
	Beach with sand exposed at low tide and submarine contour
	Coniferous woodland
	Deciduous woodland
	Marsh

Swedish 1:100 000 Map Series

R.r. 00 ⊙+++++++	State boundary with markers
+–+–+–+–	County (Län) boundary
	Commune boundary
	Parish boundary
	Village or settlement boundary
	Boundary of shooting range
	State road, dual carriageway
	State road, at least 6 m
	State road, 4.5 to 6 m
	State road, less than 4.5 m
=E4= 218	Number of main road
	Narrow road
	Narrow road, usually suitable for cars
	Residential road
	Track
	Railway, not electrified
	Railway, electrified
	Railway, double track
	Suburban or factory railway
	Station or stop with passing place and station buildings
	Electricity pylon lines with transformer (at least 20,000 volts)
	Built-up area (central area of town)
	Built-up area (residential)
	Large individual buildings
	Other large buildings
•	House or workshop
.	Hut or cabin
✚	Church with tower
¥	Hotel, motel, guest-house
⊙	Sports ground
+++++	Cemetery
⚐	Mine
	Aerodrome with surfaced runway
△00,0	Triangulation point
·00,00	Spot height, accurate
·00,0	Spot height, less accurate
·00	Spot height, least accurate
	Contours and ice surface contours (V.I. 10 metres)
	Quarry
	Low ground, sometimes water covered
	Ditto, with scattered trees
	Ditto, with woodland
	Marsh
	Marsh with scattered trees
	Marsh with trees
	Garden, orchard
	Dense forest
	Large deciduous trees in forest
	Large continuous area of scattered woods
	Scattered woodland
▲ ▲	Lapp camp, tourist camp

Danish 1:100 000 Map Series

	Motorway
E4	Main road (numbered), 2 or more lanes
10 km	Country road, kilometre stone
	Good public road
	Single lane road
	Poor road
	Track
	Path
	Vehicle ferry
Ⓢ Ⓑ Ⓣ	Railway with station, ticket office, platform
	Railway with level crossing and bridges
⊕ +	Parish church (circle denotes tower)
⊕ +	Other church (circle denotes tower)
▫	Small farm
▫	House
•	Hotel, commune office, inn, dairy, school, etc.
✿ ☥	Water-mill, windmill
⊙	Monument, landmark
△Tr St	Trigonometrical station
✈	Airport
	Lighthouse, lightship, beacon
	Embankment
	Water course
	Submarine contours 4 and 10 m.
	Deciduous woodland
	Coniferous woodland
	Rough pasture
	Marsh
	Sand or mud
	Heathland

ADMINISTRATIVE BOUNDARIES

–··–··–	County boundary
··········	Parish boundary

ABBREVIATIONS

| Gd | Gård | Farm |
| Gde | Gårde | Farms |

Dutch 1 : 50 000 and 1 : 25 000 Map Series

	Dual highway
	Metalled road, 6 m. or over
	Metalled road less than 6 m wide
	Loose- or light-surface road, less than 6 m. wide
	Local road, unmetalled
	Other unmetalled roads
	Footpath
	Double track railway, *a* embankment, *a* station
	Single track railway, *a* cut, *b* stop
	Dyke *a* from 1 to 2.5 m. high without road, *b* more than 2.5 m. high with road
	Quay less than 1 m. high *a* without road, *b* with road

	Crossings, *a* level crossing, *b* overpass, *c* underpass } viaduct
●	Church tower, tower, high dome
○	Church without tower
⊙	Church tower, tower, high dome with known coordinates
△	State Survey stone (RD)
	a Chapel, *b* Cross, *c* Sign-post
	a Windmill, *b* Water-mill
	a Small windmill, *b* Wind motor
	Pumping-engine, *a* steam, *b* motor, *c* electric

	a Oilpumping unit, *b* Signalpost, *c* Memorial, *d* Cairn
	Kilometrepost
	High tension line
.12.4	Spot height

Belgian 1 : 50 000 Map Series

COMMUNICATIONS

①	1st class road, more than 9 m
②	2nd class road, from 6–9 m
	3rd class road, less than 6 m
	3rd class road, narrow or neglected
	Earth road
At. Rép. St^on	Railway (steam) with multiple tracks
	Railway (steam) single track
	Electric railway with multiple tracks
	Electric railway, single track
Dépt	Tramway and depot
	Underpass and overpass
GV	Level crossing, tunnel
GP BC	Foot and vehicular ford, ferry and footbridge

VEGETATION

■ (green)	Woods and forests
▨ (light green)	Orchards, willows, poplars

BOUNDARIES

⊥⊥⊥⊥⊥	Province
—.—.—	Parish
60	Population number in hundreds

HUMAN FEATURES

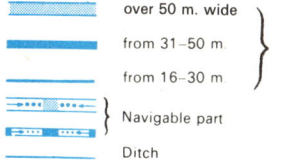

	Completely built-up area
⊙ ⊙	Trig. point (church–trig. point)
⊙	Church (no trig. point)
	In built-up areas no blue accentuation circle
† ±	Chapel, cross

	Cemetery
	Houses
	Shed or warehouse, garage
Us. Gaz.	Factory, gas tank
✳	Water-mill
○	Tower or chimney
	Radio mast
Pyl.	Ordinary pylon
	High tension cable
Ch^au eau	Water tower
	Lock

LAND AND WATER FEATURES

〜50〜	Contour lines
✺	Slag heap
	Slope
	Embankment
	Cutting } at least 1.50 m.
	River, small river, canal *over 50 m. wide*
	from 31–50 m.
	from 16–30 m.
	} Navigable part
	Ditch
E	Spring, fountain, well

ABBREVIATIONS

Anc.	Old
Charb.	Coalmine
Ch^au	Castle
Gendie	Police station

1 : 50 000 Map Series

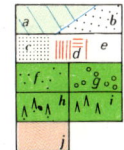

	Built-up area with main road and other roads
E10	International routes
	a Canal, *b* Canal under construction
	a Bridge, *b* Lock
	a Culvert, *b* Earth culvert, *c* Footbridge, *d* Barrage, *e* Sluice
	a Municipal hall, *b* Post, telegraph office
	Contour lines
	Municipal boundary
	a Meadow with ditches, *b* Orchard, *c* Tree nursery, *d* Glasshouses, *e* Arable land, *f* Forest of high foliated trees or brushwood, *g* High or low pine forest, *h* Heath, *i* Sand

ABBREVIATIONS

Basc br	Bascule-bridge
Dr br	Swing-bridge
Gd^r	Earth culvert
Km	Corn-mill
Oph br	Drawbridge
PK	Protestant church
pl	Pole
RK	Roman Cath. church
Sch sl	Lock
Sl	Sluice
Vbr	Footbridge
Wm	Watermill
Wt	Water tower

1 : 25 000 Map Series

	Built-up area with main road and other roads
	a Canal, *b* Canal under construction
	a Bridge, *b* Lock
	a Culvert, *b* Earth culvert, *c* Footbridge, *d* Barrage, *e* Sluice
	a Municipal hall, *b* Post office, *c* Telegraph office
	a Meadow with ditches, *b* Orchard, *c* Tree nursery, *d* Glasshouses, *e* Arable land, *f* Forest of high foliated trees or brushwood, *g* Brushwood, *h* High Pine forest, *i* Low Pine forest, *j* Heath

West European Topographical Maps

The usefulness of topographical maps in geographical studies has long been appreciated by users of the map series published by the Ordnance Survey in this country. Foreign surveys can be equally rewarding, and a selection of maps from various west European countries can provide an insight not only into the geography of the countries concerned but also into the problems and limitations of the topographical map as an instrument of expression of geographical data.

Perhaps the greatest problem that the cartographer has to face is that of the representation of relief. In earlier times this was achieved by a system of hachuring which, if well done, could produce an aesthetically pleasing result. Its greatest disadvantage lay in a lack of exactitude. It was impossible to ascertain with any accuracy the height and detailed form of mountain areas from such maps. In modern times, the contour line has become the universal answer to problems of showing detailed relief. However, its effectiveness depends upon two factors; firstly, the accuracy with which the line is drawn, and secondly, the vertical interval employed. The map series used in this book show a wide variation in this respect. The West German 1:50,000 series and the French 1:25,000 series show an interesting use of contours and form lines. On both types of map a vertical interval of 10 metres is used for the contours, but on gentle slopes where more space is available the information provided by the contours is frequently supplemented by form lines drawn at 5 metre and 2·5 metre intervals. Other series have a less flexible system. The Dutch maps use a vertical interval of 5 metres, and the French 1:50,000 series one of 10 metres. In fact, with the exception of the Norwegian and Swiss maps, with their contour intervals of 30 and 20 metres, all the other series represented in the book use a vertical interval which is less than the 50 feet employed on our own 1:63,360 Ordnance Survey maps. Even so, the limitations of contours in the recognition of minor relief forms such as river terraces can be appreciated from a study of a number of the extracts. The representation of relief also involves the question of legibility as well as accuracy. One of the devices employed to increase this quality is that of hill shading. By this method the general layout of the relief can be seen before detailed investigation of contours is undertaken. Three of the map series represented in this book provide good examples of this technique, namely the French 1:50,000 the West German 1:50,000 (in some Länder) and the Swiss 1:50,000. Of these, the Swiss maps are among the finest produced in Europe. It is remarkable how landscapes with such complexity of relief become readily understandable through the use of finely toned shadows. The Swiss survey also illustrates another technique of the map maker, namely the representation of steep cliffs by rock drawing. The finely drawn detail on the Engadine and Gorner Glacier extracts are models of what can be achieved.

Representation of land use is another important aspect to be considered in attempting to interpret human geography from a topographical map. In most cases surveys are inadequate in this respect, although most represent an advance on the limited amount of information provided by the maps of the Ordnance Survey. The British 1:63,360 maps distinguish between woodland of two types, rough pasture (which can vary greatly) and the buildings, roads and other works of man. There is little distinction between types of farming apart from orchards and glasshouses. The distinction between arable land and permanent pasture thus becomes a matter of deduction and inference from location. By comparison, the West German 1:50,000 maps cover the same categories as the Ordnance Survey maps but have additional symbols for vineyards and hop gardens. The French 1:50,000 survey has a similar range of land use symbols. The most effective series in this respect are the Dutch 1:50,000 and 1:25,000 maps. Reference to the appropriate key sheets will show the wide range of land use symbols employed, possibly a natural reflection of the high value that the Dutch place upon their land.

It should be borne in mind that the key sheets on pages 10, 11, 94, and 95 include only those symbols required for the interpretation of the various map extracts. The keys on the full map sheets give additional symbols. These, in fact, show a wide variation in the amount of information that they provide. For example, the relatively small amount of information provided by the Norwegian 1:50,000 maps may be compared with the lengthy list of conventional signs used on the Swedish, Dutch, West German and Swiss maps at the same scale. These differences, of course, reflect not only the aspirations of the cartographers but also the varying complexity of the landscapes being portrayed. Some of the map keys are noticeably lacking in information about many symbols which appear on the map sheets. This is true of the French maps, which are also made more difficult to read on account of the frequent use of abbreviations on the maps, the meanings of which are not given in the keys.

The use of a grid system for map references is familiar to users of the Ordnance Survey maps. A similar practice is common throughout Europe, and the same kilometre square size is used for the grid. Usually a full grid system is provided, while in some cases, notably the French and most West German maps, reference numbers are provided in the margins but no grid lines drawn on the maps. In the cases of the Norwegian 1:100,000, Danish 1:100,000 and Belgian 1:50,000 series no system of either grid squares or numbering is employed.

In using the various west European map series one is struck by the considerable variation in standards and styles of lettering employed on the map sheets. Poor legibility reduces the value of many maps. This is true of the Norwegian 1:50,000 series, on which heavy type frequently obscures significant detail. These considerations of legibility have in part determined the choice of study areas, for in many parts of Europe landscapes of great interest are still only covered by maps which have limited value to the geographer. The use of colour may similarly affect the legibility and usefulness of a map series. The Swiss sheets are restrained and economical in this respect, but nevertheless manage to portray a difficult topography with success. Other maps employ more colours, notably those of the Netherlands and Belgium. The maps of the latter country suffer from an over-use of solid black shading for built up areas. This obscures much significant detail of relief etc., and is an unsatisfactory answer to the difficult problem of representing urban areas.

Exercises

1. To what extent would you subscribe to the dictum that what is unmappable is not geography? (S.U.J.B.)
2. How far are the considerations of legibility and the provision of detailed information compatible in the production of topographical maps? On which of the map extracts included in the book do you consider the problem to have been most effectively solved?
3. What information do you consider might be added to the following maps to increase their usefulness to the geographer: *(a)* Aurland; *(b)* Geestmerambacht; *(c)* Duisburg; *(d)* Marseilles?
4. Assess the problems of representing relief cartographically. (W.J.E.C.)
5. Take a single grid square on an Ordnance Survey 2½ inch: 1 mile map, and draw maps to show the same area in the style of any four European map series.
6. Which of the map series included in the book do you consider to be of most value as an aid to the study of *(a)* landforms; *(b)* agricultural geography; *(c)* industrial geography? Justify your choice.
7. To what extent is the choice of land use symbols appearing on the various national map series a reflection of the geography of these countries?
8. Compare the cartographic techniques used on the Copenhagen map extract with those employed in portraying a British city of comparable size on the 1 inch : 1 mile (7th series) maps of the Ordnance Survey. Bear in mind scale differences when making your critical assessment.
9. Compare and contrast the cartographic techniques employed on the Dutch 1 : 25,000, the French 1 : 25,000 and the Ordnance Survey 1 : 25,000 map series. Organise your answer under the following headings: representation of relief, land use, settlement, communications, and aesthetic considerations.
10. Make a critical assessment of the different ways of portraying land use on the Dutch and West German 1 : 50,000 map series.
11. To what extent do aerial photographs provide additional data which is not shown on the maps?
12. Comment on the relative merits and shortcomings of oblique and vertical air photographs for purposes of geographical interpretation.

Further reading

DEFFONTAINES, P. and DELAMARRE, M. J. *Atlas Aërien, France*. Vols. I–V, Librairie Gallimard, 1955–64.
DICKINSON, G. C. *Maps and Air Photographs*, E. J. Arnold, 1968.
DURY, G. H. *Map Interpretation*, Pitman, 1960.
GARNETT, A. *The Geographical Interpretation of Topographical Maps*, Harrap, 1953.
HINKS, A. R. *Maps and Survey*, Cambridge U.P., 1944.
RAISZ, E. *Principles of Cartography*, McGraw-Hill, 1962.
SMITH, M. T. U. *Aerial Photographs and their Application*, Appleton-Century, 1943.
SYLVESTER, D. *Map and Landscape*, Philip, 1952.
WALKER, F. *Geography from the Air*, Methuen, 1953.
ST. JOSEPH, J. K. S., Ed., *The Uses of Air Photography*, John Baker, 1966.

Study 1
AURLAND
SOGN and FJORDANE NORWAY

A Fjord Coast

Extract From Map Sheet 1416 IV. Aurland.
Norwegian 1:50,000 Series

Published 1952.
Vertical interval of contours 30 metres.

The map extract printed by permission of the Geographical Survey of Norway.

Map 1

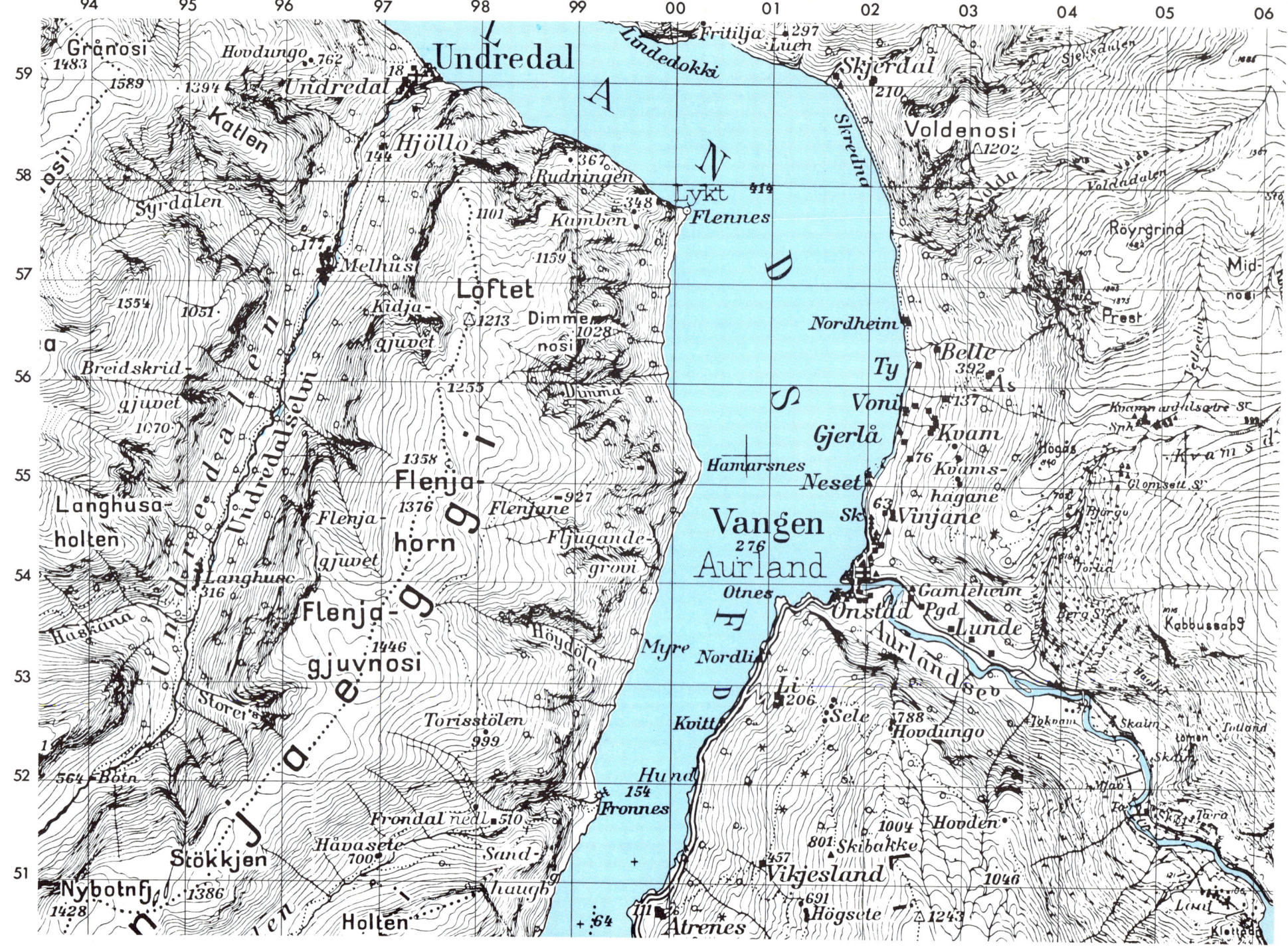

Photograph 1. Aurlandsfjord. View of the fjord slopes to the north of the Aurland River. The village of Aurland is seen at the mouth of river.

Mittet Photo A/S, Oslo.

The two principal series of Norwegian topographical maps are those at scales of 1:50,000 and 1:100,000. The Svolvær extract (Study 2) is an example of the older *gradteig* sheets which are based on late 19th-century surveys with subsequent revisions. The Aurlandsfjord study uses an extract from one of the 1:50,000 'tourist' sheets which were introduced in 1943.

Fjord coasts

Fjords may be described as long, narrow, steep-sided inlets of the sea penetrating in a rectilinear pattern of branching arms far into upland coastal regions. True fjords are found along the edges of mountainous areas which have been subject to glaciation, and it is thus held that they have resulted from former glaciers deeply eroding preglacial river valleys which in turn were probably guided by tectonic weaknesses. Many fjords are characterised by extremely great depths and yet are relatively shallow near their mouths. For example, Sogne Fjord, of which Aurlandsfjord is a branch, reaches depths of 4,000 feet, considerably deeper than the floor of the North Sea into which it opens, and yet is only about 500 feet deep at its mouth.

The formation of fjords has long been a subject of controversy. For example, they have been attributed to faulting on account of their rectilinear plan in many areas, but this fails to explain their restricted distribution to glaciated regions. Thus, while fjords are now generally accepted as being partially submerged glaciated valleys, their great depth and the presence of a threshold of apparently solid rock has led to much discussion as to their detailed mode of formation. Such a form implies a vast amount of glacial overdeepening of the inner parts of the fjord. It is necessary to assume that the inner parts of the pre-glacial valleys were greatly eroded as the glaciers flowed steeply down from the nearby ice-caps but were much less deeply cut where the ice entered the sea. It has been suggested by Cailleux that variations in the depth of frozen ground before the advance of the ice might be a significant factor in this respect, the ground being less deeply frozen and shattered near the sea than inland and thus less easily eroded by the glaciers. (A. Cailleux. 'Polissage et Surcreusement Glaciaires dans l'Hypothèse de Boyé'. *Revue de Géomorphologie Dynamique, 3*, 1952.)

Aurlandsfjord

Aurlandsfjord is a southern arm of Sogne Fjord and lies about 100 miles from the open sea (fig. 2). Even at this distance from the main fjord entrance a sounding of 414 metres is indicated. The walls of the fjord are extremely steep, especially on the western side where gradients in excess of 1 in 2 are encountered. This side of the fjord is broken by two hanging valleys. Undre-

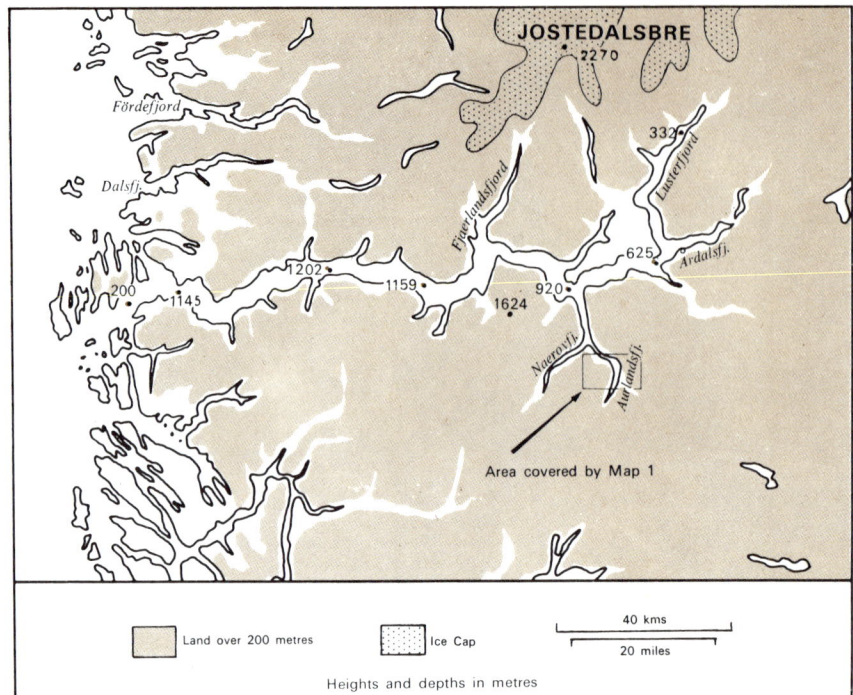

Figure 2. Sogne Fjord.

dal and Frondal, although in the case of the latter the typical glaciated form is modified by a deeply incised post-glacial stream valley. The floor level of Undredal corresponds closely with the level of submergence of the fjord valley, but the stream occupying Frondal plunges steeply down into the fjord and has built out the small deltaic platform on which the saw mill at Fronnes is sited (993519). On the opposite shore the mouth of another hanging valley, Skjerdal, may also be noted. The eastern side of the fjord is generally less steep, apart from the slopes below Voldenosi (030584), and is also breached by the valley of the Aurlandselv. Elsewhere small streams in incipient valleys plunge precipitously down from the mountain crags.

Settlement, occupations and communications

The settlement of the area shows a close correlation with topography both in amount and distribution. Nucleation occurs at Aurland/Onstad (0254), Undredal (9759) and to a much lesser degree on the more gentle slopes at Kvam (0255). These villages have populations of 484, 198 and 130 respectively. Elsewhere scattered farms and houses take advantage of the limited number of safe and suitable sites for building offered by the terrain, for rock and snow avalanches and landslips are a constant threat to property. The highest parts of the area are, of course, devoid of settlement.

The means of livelihood in fjord areas such as Aurlandsfjord is based essentially on farming, tourism, forestry and fishing, but clear distinctions cannot be drawn. Fishing, which is far less important than along the open coast, and forestry, which attains its maximum importance in south-east Norway, are merely supplements to what is essentially a farming economy, and tourism in West Norway is markedly seasonal.

Aurland. Principal occupations of the working population
Based on the 1960 Census[1]

Agriculture and Forestry	233	30.4%
Building and Construction	163	21.1%
Service Trades and Professions	157	20.4%
Transport and Communications	106	13.8%
Industry	98	12.7%
Administration	9	1.1%

[1] *Tellingsresulter-Tilbakegående Tall-Prognoser. Aurland, No. 1412. Statistisk Sentralbyrå. Oslo. 1961.*
(Note: The commune of Aurland extends beyond the limits of the map extract).

As can be seen from these figures, agriculture is the chief means of livelihood, but the figures fail to reveal the degree to which the agricultural economy is supplemented by forestry and fishing. The farms in the area are generally small, owner-occupied and divided into what is known as the *innmark* and *utmark*. The former consists of small enclosed fields supporting crops of oats, barley and hay, while the latter, the outfield, takes the form of sæter grazing in these fjord districts. The typical sæter pastures with their collection of small huts such as Kvammardalsætre (049557) and Glomsett Sæter (046552) generally lie just above the treeline so that timber is available, but on the least accessible of the fjord slopes they are found at much lower altitudes as at Fritilja (003595), Luen (011594), Rudningen (989583) and Kamben (996577). The sæters lie at varying distances from the farmsteads to which they are linked by rough trackways. Notice the interesting clusters of sæter buildings at Melhus (965571) and Langhusc (952540) in Undredal. The pattern of transhumance or *seterdrift* varies widely from area to area both in timing and duration. In some cases a single sæter may be used, while in other instances a farmer may make use of several sæters during the summer. The high level grazing above Aurlandsfjord is used for about 3 months each year.

The absence of an integrated communication system is a striking feature of the area. A secondary road runs along part of the eastern side of the fjord and links Aurland with the head of the fjord which lies just beyond the map extract. From there the famous Flåm Railway climbs in a series of spirals to join the Oslo/Bergen Railway at Myrdal, so that Aurlandsfjord is less isolated than many in West Norway. A minor cul-de-sac road leads eastwards from Aurland to small hamlets and farms in the lower part of Aurlandsdal. The western side of the fjord is virtually devoid of roads and the village of Undredal relies entirely upon boats for its links with outside areas, a situation that is by no means uncommon among the fjord communities.

Fjord districts such as Aurlandsfjord constitute some of the most distinctive landscapes in western Europe. The relief of these areas provides probably the most spectacular example of glacial erosion, and the human occupancy of the fjords shows a close adjustment to the conditions imposed by a unique and often difficult environment.

Abbreviations

In addition to the key symbols given on page 10 the following abbreviations occur on the map:

Bg—Berg Hill; mountain   *Pgd—Prestegård* Vicarage
Ev—Elv River   *Sk—Skole* School
Fj—Fjell Mountain   *Sph—Sportshytte* Sports Cabin
Nedl—Nedlagt Abandoned   *Sr—Seter* Saeter

Exercises

1. Draw a sketch section from the spur Katlen (955585) to the slopes of Kabbussaberg (052542). Estimate the depth of the fjord at the point where it is crossed by the section line and extend the valley sides to give an approximate submarine profile. Mark the treeline on your section and label the landforms shown.

2. 'Where the larger side valleys meet the main fjord valley there are generally a cluster of houses and a pier which act as a focal point. . . . Settlement on the fjord sides takes three main forms; it may climb an embayment of gentler slope, it may follow a raised beach, or it may occur as isolated units on shelves high up on the fjord sides or on the floors of side valleys which "hang" to the main valley.' A. C. O'Dell, *The Scandinavian World*.
   How far do you consider this description to be applicable to the settlement of Aurlandsfjord?

3. 'Settlement shows a close correlation with topography both in amount and distribution.' With the aid of a map showing the distribution of both permanent settlement and sæters, amplify this statement.

4. Construct two frequency curves to show the relationship between altitude and the distribution of *(a)* sæters and *(b)* permanent settlement. Comment on your result.

Further reading

EVANS, E. E. 'Transhumance in Europe', *Geography* **25**, no 4, 1940.
GREFFIER, M. J. *Le Pays d'Aurland dans la Région du Sognefjord*. Bull. de l'Ass. des Géog. Français, 1952.
GREGORY, J. W. *The Origin and Nature of Fjords*, Murray, 1913.
MEAD, W. R. *An Economic Geography of the Scandinavian States and Finland*, London U.P., 2nd Edition, 1968, chapter 7.
MEAD, W. R. 'Sogn and Fjordane in the fjord economy of western Norway', *Economic Geography* **23**, 1947.
O'DELL, A. C. *The Scandinavian World*, Longmans, 1957, chapter 10.
STRØM, K. M. 'The geomorphology of Norway', *Geographical Journal* **112**, 1948.

Study 2
SVOLVAER
NORDLAND
NORWAY

A Lofoten Fishing Town

Extract From Map Sheet K10.
Svolvær. Norwegian
1:100,000 Series.

First published 1902.
Revised in the field 1956.
Roads up-to-date 1958.
Vertical interval of contours
30 metres.
Note. Longitude readings give
the number of degrees east
of the Oslo meridian. (Oslo
meridian = 10°-43'-22.5"
east of Greenwich.)

*The map extract printed by
permission of the Geographical
Survey of Norway.*

Map 2

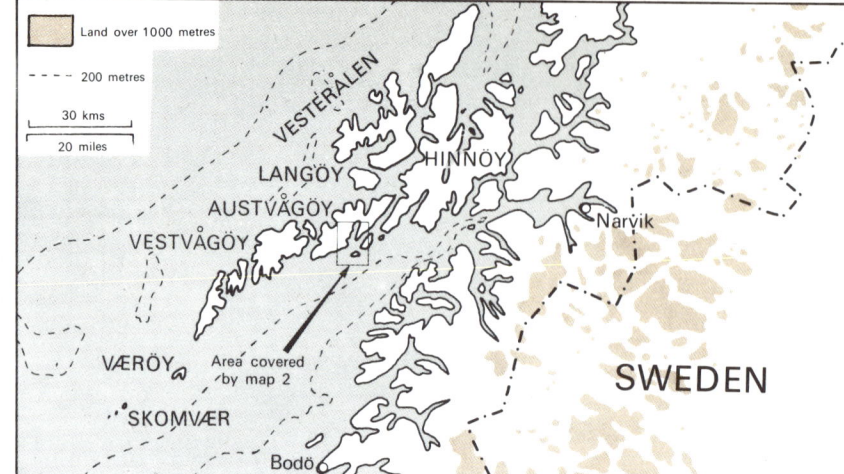

Figure 3. The Lofoten Islands.

The Lofoten Islands are among some 150,000 islands which border the coast of Norway. The group stretches south-west for about 100 miles from Hinnöy to the rocky outpost of Skomvær, and, like the Vesterålen group to the north, lies on a submarine ridge which separates Vestfjord from the North Atlantic. The map extract shows the southern part of Austvågöy together with smaller islands in the vicinity of the small town of Svolvær. The area portrayed lies about 120 miles within the Arctic Circle.

Relief features of the Svolvær district

The land in the area covered by the map extract rises with extraordinary steepness to a maximum height of 1,062 metres. The southern slopes of the island of Lille Molla, for example, exceed 45° and comparably steep slopes can be found at many other points in the area. The plutonic rocks of the district have been deeply dissected by glacial erosion to produce a landscape of sharp, rugged peaks and narrow ridges or arêtes. These pyramid peaks are denoted by the term *Tind* (abb. *Td.*) which occurs frequently on the map extract. The mountains are deeply cut by corries and the extract provides several examples of these features with their small lakes and steep bounding walls. It will be noted that whereas corries are found only at high elevations in the mountain areas further south in Europe, in this arctic region they occur close to, or even at, sea-level as well as at higher levels. The figures on the various corrie lakes indicate the surface height of the lakes, so that it is

Photograph 2. Svolvær. Lofoten. Notice the nature of the strandflat upon which Svolvær is built and the steepness of the distant peaks.

Widerøe's Flyveselskap og Polarfly A/S, Oslo.

reasonable to suppose that the floor of Helle-sæter Vand (16 metres and 2 metres) lies below sea-level. It is generally believed that during the latter stages of the Quaternary glaciation the Lofoten Islands supported a local ice-cap detached from the main mass of inland ice on the Scandinavian Peninsula to the east. It is interesting to note that the map shows permanent ice and snow on the flanks of Langstrandtindene to the east of Östnes Fjord. Elsewhere the mountains are less high and fail to reach the level of permanent snow, although in such high latitudes there is, of course, a long duration of snow cover.

A striking feature of both the map and photograph is the fringe of low, flat ground just above sea-level. This rock platform which is found along much of the coast of West Norway is known as the strandflat. In addition to the fringe of low ground at the foot of the mountains the strandflat is also represented by the multitude of small, low islands which rise only just above sea-level and the rocks which lie just below sea-level. Norwegians refer to the 'dry' and 'wet' strandflat to denote those parts of the platform which lie just above or just below sea-level. The various rock formations of the strandflat are of vital significance to the maritime communities of Norway's west coast and figure prominently in the local vocabulary. The following terms signify particular features of the strandflat and many occur as part of the local names on the map extract.

Bo	Shoal near the surface	*Holme* (abb. *Hl.*)	Small island
Brake	Rock with heavy breakers	*Klakke*	Shoal or fishing ground
Bråt	Shoal with breakers	*Öy* or *Ö*	Island or islet
Drag	Long rock	*Skjær* (abb. *Skj.*)	Small rock, skerry, or shelf
Fall	Shoal with breakers	*Slu*	Long skerry below water
Fles	Flat skerry; low-lying island	*Stabbe*	High rock; stack
Flu	Skerry showing at low tide	*Tare*	Seaweed seen at low tide.

(It should be noted that where these terms are found on the map sheet they occur in the definitive form ending in 'et', 'a', or 'en'.)

The date and mode of formation of the strandflat is still a topic of controversy. One of the most detailed studies of the feature is that of Fridtjof Nansen, who considered that it was produced by marine denudation aided by sub-aerial frost action. (F. Nansen, *The Strandflat and Isostasy,* Oslo, 1922.) Nansen also believed that the strandflat consisted of three platforms with inner edges at *c.* 25 feet, 50–60 feet and 100–130 feet above the present sea-level. The vertical interval of the map is, of course, inadequate for any determination of these subdivisions. A more recent explanation is that of the German geomorphologist Wolf Tietze, who envisages planation by shelf-ice on a tidal coastline. Erosion is thought to have resulted from the former movement of the ice due to tidal fluctuations. (W. Tietze, 'Ein Beitrag zum geomorphologischen Problem der Strandflate', *Petermanns Geographische Mitteilungen,* **106**, 1962.) Notice on the map sheet the way in which a broken line indicates water that is dangerous for shipping. This 'danger line' encloses much of the submerged portion of the strandflat. From the limited number of depths marked on the map it would seem that a deep channel, Höla (156 metres deep at one point), lies about two miles offshore from Svolvær. This is probably a submerged continuation of Östnes Fjord which extends across the strandflat.

Climate and vegetation

Since the Lofoten Islands lie within the Arctic Circle (Svolvær 68°15′ N.) the climate is, as would be expected, very severe in winter. However, the North Atlantic Drift has a pronounced ameliorating effect on winter temperatures along the whole of the west coast of the country, so that the littoral zone of North Norway has in fact the highest temperature anomaly, not only in Europe, but in the world. That is to say, if one finds the average temperature for a particular line of latitude it is then possible to examine deviations from the mean for particular places along that parallel. This deviation is known as the 'thermal anomaly', and near the Lofotens there is a record positive anomaly of 25·5°C. in January.

The mean January temperature for Svolvær is −0·7°C, which is less cold than the mean January temperature of Oslo (−4·2°C) almost 600 miles to the south. Winter temperatures in Norway in fact decrease more rapidly inland than northwards. The arctic position of the Lofotens is more apparent in summer when the mean July temperature of Svolvær is only 11·9°C. Total annual precipitation is 23·4 inches with an all-seasonal distribution and much of it in the form of snow. Mention should also be made of the frequent gales which are a feature of the weather of the Lofoten district and which often occur during the winter fishing season. The arctic position of the islands means that they experience the 'midnight sun' effect in summer and a period of continuous and oppressive darkness in winter.

These climatic conditions are reflected in the natural vegetation of the area covered by the map. The combination of short growing season and poor, thin soils results in an absence of tree cover over much of the area. As can be appreciated from photograph 2, these outer coastal districts are generally bare and windswept, although scattered patches of deciduous trees (probably birch) are marked on the lower, more gentle slopes and rise to heights of *c.* 150 metres. (This may be compared with the tree-line at *c.* 800 metres in the Aurland district. See Study 1.) The valley floors and much of the strandflat appear to be badly drained, as is indicated by the frequent occurrence of the symbol denoting marsh. The lingering snow cover and the slight gradients of the strandflat are probably significant factors in this respect.

Settlement and occupations

The most striking feature of the settlement pattern is the marked concentration of population along the coast. Almost all the settlement lies on the strandflat. Much of the building is scattered, and the only nucleated settlement is Svolvær on the south coast of Austvågöy. In 1960 Svolvær had a modest population total of 3,812, but this figure shows marked seasonal fluctuations according to the movements of the fleets of small fishing vessels. At the height of the Lofoten fishing season as many as 10,000 fishermen move into the region from all parts of the north and west coasts of Norway so that 'some villages have up to ten times the off-season population' (Tore Sund). In the Lofoten Islands as a whole about three times as many people have fishing for their chief occupation as farming, although a combination of fishing and farming is a common means of livelihood. In the county of Nordland 28% of the working population has more than one occupation. Only very rarely is fishing subordinate to farming.

The map extract gives little information about farming. Farmsteads are shown at various points along the strandflat as, for example, along the shores of Östnes Fjord and on the eastern shore of Lille Molla. Two sæters, Bergs Sæter and Helle Sæter, are shown on the shores of Svolværvand and Vatterfjordpollen respectively. Agricultural emphasis in such an area, with its lack of soil, steep rocky slopes and severe climate must clearly be on livestock and the growing of fodder crops.

The sea, with its rich fisheries in this area, offers greater possibilities for making a livelihood than the land. The indented coast with its numerous bays and inlets provides many sheltered harbours for small vessels, but on the other hand an indication of the difficulties of navigation is suggested by the numerous marker lights (*Lykt,* abb. *Lkt* = a light), and the multitude of small islands, rocks and shoals. Strong tidal currents run through the narrow channels, and frequent storms add to the hazards of navigation. The Lofoten shores are visited by shoals of arctic-water fish such as cod, saithe, haddock and ling. The cod fishing is particularly important during the period January to April, and the Lofoten Banks rank as one of the most important fishing grounds in Europe. Unfortunately the area lies distant from markets and the bulk of the catch must therefore be dried *(stockfisk)* or salted *(klipfisk).* Of the total catch of Lofoten cod almost 90% is dried and salted for South American and Mediterranean markets, and only 10% sold fresh or frozen. A close examination of photograph 2 shows the wooden scaffolds on which the fish are hung to dry. They are to be found, for example, on the small islet beyond Svolvær church. Although the map provides no specific information, it may be assumed that many of the larger buildings along the quays of Svolvær are used for the processing, freezing, packeting and marketing of fish, the production of fish-meal, fish-oil and fertilisers, or the repair of boats and fishing equipment.

In conclusion it may be said that the Lofoten Islands constitute a very difficult and hostile environment. The population in the map area is of low density and unevenly distributed. Few roads are shown, and, as in many districts in North Norway, the chief means of communication in the area is by the sea. Svolvær itself has daily calls from the express coastal steamers *(Hurtigruten)* travelling both north to Tromsö, Hammerfest and Kirkenes and south to Bodö, Trondheim and Bergen. The economic resources of these northern islands are extremely limited and life in high latitudes can never be easy. Agriculture provides only poor returns, and fishing, the chief occupation, constitutes a hazardous and uncertain livelihood.

Glossary of geographical terms

The following terms and their abbreviations occur frequently on the map extract.

Dal Valley
Fj., Fjell Mountain
Fd., Fjord Fjord
Poll Creek

Vaag Inlet or bay
Vær Fishing village
Vd., Vand, Vatn Lake
Vik Bay

Exercises

1. Calculate the number of days of continuous darkness in winter at *(a)* Svolvær (68°15′ N), *(b)* Tromsö (69°40′ N) and *(c)* Hammerfest (70°33′ N). Suggest how this period of continuous darkness affects the life of North Norway.
2. Identify the observation point, direction of view (full circle bearing) and angle of view of photograph 2. Find the names of features A, B, C and D marked on the photograph.
3. From a careful examination of both the map extract and the photograph write a description of Svolvær. The description, which should be illustrated with an annotated sketch map, should include reference to the site, the density and arrangement of buildings and the type of buildings in the town.
4. 'North Norway would be practically uninhabited without its rich marine resources' (Axel Sømme). Discuss.

Further reading

ALGÅRD, G. 'A farm in northern Norway', *Geographical Magazine,* **27,** no 4, 1954.
MEAD, W. R. *An Economic Geography of the Scandinavian States and Finland,* London U.P., 2nd Edition, 1968, chapter 8.
MILLWARD, R. *Scandinavian Lands,* Macmillan, 1964, chapter 11.
Norway, vols I and II Naval Intelligence Geographical Handbook Series, 1943.
O'DELL, A. C. *The Scandinavian World,* Longmans, 1957, chapters 10 and 17.
SØMME, A., ed. 'The Geography of Norden', Heinemann, 1961, chapter 11.
SUND, T. and SØMME, A. *Norway in Maps,* A. S. John Greigs Boktrykkert, Bergen, 1947.
VORREN, Ø., ed. *Norway North of* 65, Allen and Unwin, 1961.

Study 3
KIRUNA NORRBOTTEN SWEDEN

An Arctic Mining Settlement.

Extract from Map Sheet 29 J. Kiruna. Swedish 1:100,000 Series.

Surveyed 1959-60.
Published 1961.
Lines of latitude and longitude at 0°-10' intervals.
Vertical interval of contours 10 metres.

Reprinted from the topographic map Geographical Survey Office Sweden. Release nr 6767, SRA, Vällingby 1, Sweden.

22 **Map 3**

Sweden has map coverage at scales of 1:50,000, 1:100,000 and 1:250,000. The map extract provides an example of the new, coloured 1:100,000 sheets which are replacing the older, hachured editions at that scale. Within the limitations imposed by a scale of 1:100,000 these new maps give a quite detailed representation of the Swedish topography in a style which is both legible and æsthetically satisfying.

Kiruna is one of the largest centres of population in Arctic Europe and is situated at a higher altitude than any other town in Scandinavia. It lies among the forests of Norrbotten, Sweden's northernmost *län* or county, almost 900 miles north of Stockholm by rail and about 100 miles north of the Arctic Circle, a latitude equivalent to northern Alaska or the Siberian tundra. The town stands on the railway between Luleå on the Bothnian coast and Narvik on the Norwegian coast, but is poorly served by roads. It can only be approached by route 98, a branch road which terminates in the town and carries traffic from North Norway via Karesuando and, more particularly, from the more southerly districts of Sweden via Gällivare. The minor roads shown on the map all terminate a short distance beyond the map area and merely link Kiruna with small surrounding settlements.

Relief and drainage

The Scandinavian Peninsula consists of a basement of extremely ancient pre-Cambrian rocks which had been folded and reduced to a peneplain even before Palaeozoic times. On top of this peneplain, known as the Baltic Shield, sediments were deposited during Cambrian and Silurian times and folded in late Silurian times into the Caledonian mountain system. The Caledonian mountains in their turn were reduced to a peneplain, and their present elevation is due to an epeirogenic uplift in late Tertiary times. The present relief of the Scandinavian peninsula is thus the result of a complex polycyclic erosional history. To the east of the main watershed a series of uplifted erosion surfaces dominate the landscape. Sten Rudberg uses the term 'Monadnock Plain' to describe the landscape of inner Norrbotten with its isolated hills rising above the plateaux surfaces.

The map extract shows a dissected plateau with a series of peaks rising up above the general level of the region. Notable among such peaks are Aptasvaara (614 metres), Kirunavaara (*c.* 930 metres), Luossavaara (723 metres), Sakkaravaara (573 metres) and Kurravaara (*c.* 590 metres). Gently sloping surfaces are also evident, and at many points the direction of drainage appears to be indeterminate, as is indicated by the numerous marsh areas and temporary lakes. The pre-Cambrian rocks of the district consist of granites, porphyries, leptites and gneisses, but due to the complicated

Photograph 3. Kiruna and the Kirunavaara iron working. View from Luossavaara.

L.K.A.B. Fotografi, Stockholm, Börje Rönnberg.

erosional history there is little or no correlation between relief and geology.

The Quaternary glaciation produced considerable modifications to the relief and drainage of the area. North Sweden was not free of ice until c. 6500 B.C. (the Ancylus Lake period) and consequently the results of glaciation have been relatively little modified by post-glacial weathering and erosion. Much of the Baltic Shield is covered with a hummocky deposit of coarse morainic and fluvioglacial material which is deficient in lime and has a permafrost layer about 1 yard below the surface. Gley soils have developed and support a cover of poor forest which in the Kiruna district consists chiefly of stunted birches and scrub. Only along the Torneälv valley is there any indication of coniferous forest. Due to the impermeability of the soil and the extensive areas of slight gradient, many pockets of marsh and swamp may be noted (horizontal brown shading on the map).

Kiruna lies between two of the largest rivers in North Sweden, the Torneälv (älv = a river) and the Kalixälv (the latter lies just beyond the southern edge of the extract). The Torneälv, to the north-east of Kiruna, is more than 1 km wide in this area and really forms the southern end of the 80 mile long Lake Torneträsk, which stretches from the Norwegian frontier. These rivers are two of a series of roughly parallel, consequent rivers which rise on the high *fjäll* and drop steeply in a south-east direction to the Gulf of Bothnia. They have all been rejuvenated as a result of post-glacial isostatic uplift which, in the case of North Sweden, is estimated to have been as much as 500–700 feet. In the vicinity of Luleå isostatic uplift is still continuing at a rate of 1 cm (0·4 inches) per year, although the actual rise of the land in relation to the sea is slightly less due to an eustatic rise of sea-level. The Swedish rivers are therefore characterised by irregular, ungraded longitudinal profiles with numerous falls and rapids.

The view from the summit of the hill on which Kiruna is built is described by Noel Watts as follows: 'From this point to the north nothing is to be seen but flat swampy land covered with small bushes and scrub. The view westwards is somewhat similar except that the horizon is dominated by a range of snow-covered mountains. It is when one looks south that the reason for the existence of such a large community in this barren and inhospitable land becomes apparent. Below the station lies a long lake and on its further shore another hill rises to a considerable height. It is split in half by a great gash many hundreds of feet deep and in this gash is the world-famous iron-ore mine. Every person in Kiruna depends directly or indirectly on this great man-made hole for his or her living.'

The iron working of Kiruna

The existence of ore deposits at Kiruna was known as early as the seventeenth century, but no attempt at exploitation was made until 1890, when the company of Luossavaara-Kiirunavaara Aktiebolag (generally known as L.K.A.B.) began the opening up of the Kiruna mines. The problems to be faced were immense. A labour force had to be attracted to this desolate region and a completely new settlement built to house the mining community. Facilities had to be established to allow the continuation of mining throughout the long arctic winter, and, most important of all, a railway had to be driven for more than 100 miles over the mountains to the Norwegian coast where an export port could be established. Luleå was unsuitable as the main outlet for the ore, since it is normally closed by ice from November to May, but the Norwegian coast remains ice-free in winter as a result of the North Atlantic Drift. (See Study 2.)

In 1902 a railway was completed from Kiruna to Narvik on the Norwegian coast, descending through a series of great gorges and tunnels to the sea at Ofot Fjord. At the same time a line was constructed to connect with the older mining centre of Malberget (Gällivare) which had already been linked in 1888 with Luleå. The map extract shows that the Ofot Railway, as it is known, is a single-track electrified line flanked with a power cable carrying more than 20,000 volts.

The iron deposit at Kiruna occurs as an enormous slab about $2\frac{1}{2}$ miles long and 100 yards wide, running north-south through Kirunavaara and pitching eastwards at an angle of $40°–75°$. Some sixty years of opencast mining have split the mountain with a huge terraced trench which extends down almost to the level of Lake Luossajärvi. Since 1962 all mining has been underground, and test drills have shown that the ore body extends down to at least 3,300 ft below the surface. The deposit continues northwards under the lake to Luossavaara where a similar, though much smaller, trench has been cut into the mountain. The symbol indicating a mine or quarry also appears on the map at Tuolluvaara to the east of Kiruna. This is a relatively small, privately owned iron working (as opposed to the larger L.K.A.B. mines of Kirunavaara and Luossavaara which are state-owned).

At a scale of 1:100,000 the map extract is unable to provide much information about the iron workings. However, it does show how the three mines have been connected to the main railway by a system of branch lines. In the case of Kirunavaara, zones of both old and new industry are marked. (*G.la ind.omr.* and *Nya industriomr.* respectively). The sketch map gives a more detailed picture of the workings. The central block (*Centralanläggingen*) which is just visible beyond Kirunavaara in the photograph consists of the main hoisting gear together with a concentrating and pelletizing plant constructed in 1965. The new lakeside industrial zone includes a thirteen-storey administrative block which can also be clearly seen in photograph 3.

The ore mineral of the Kiruna district is magnetite, although hematite occurs in small quantities. The iron content is very high (60–70%), but the ore is phosphoric, a fact which rendered it unusable until after the invention of the Thomas steel converter (Basic Bessemer) in 1879. This single technical innovation transformed the geography of northern Sweden.

At the present time there is an almost constant flow of crushed ore from Kiruna and Malmberget to the exporting ports of Narvik and Luleå. At peak periods as many as 32 trains, each carrying over 2,000 tons of ore, leave Kiruna for Narvik every 24 hours. This section of line in fact carries a greater tonnage per kilometre than any other railway in the world, and day and night the ore is constantly moving to the coast. Even during the most severe spells of winter weather the railway is kept open by snow ploughs, but snow-sheds and drift-fences are essential along the exposed sections of line. In 1965 the Kiruna mines produced 15·7 million tons of ore (Kirunavaara 14·6 million tons, Luossavaara 0·5, and Tuolluvaara 0·6). In addition, Malmberget produced 4·6 million tons, giving a total of 20·3 million tons. Of this, 16·1 million tons were exported via Narvik, 3·6 via Luleå, and 9·6 carried by rail to southern Sweden. West Germany is the biggest importer of ore from Norrbotten, followed by Great Britain and Belgium. Relatively small amounts are sent to U.S.A., France, The Netherlands and Italy.

Settlement of the Kiruna district

The actual urban district of Kiruna covers a vast area. It is in fact the largest town in area in the world (5,539 square miles), although the total population is only 28,000 of which about 22,000 people live in the actual settlement of Kiruna, which is referred to as Kiruna C. In 1966, 3,600 workers were employed in the Kirunavaara and Luossavaara mines, and a further 300 in the Tuolluvaara working. Various incentives are offered to attract and maintain such a labour force in this remote arctic district. Wages are 25% higher than in central Sweden for the equivalent work, and the standards of housing and amenities are as high as in any other part of the country. The problem of isolation and the great distance from the main

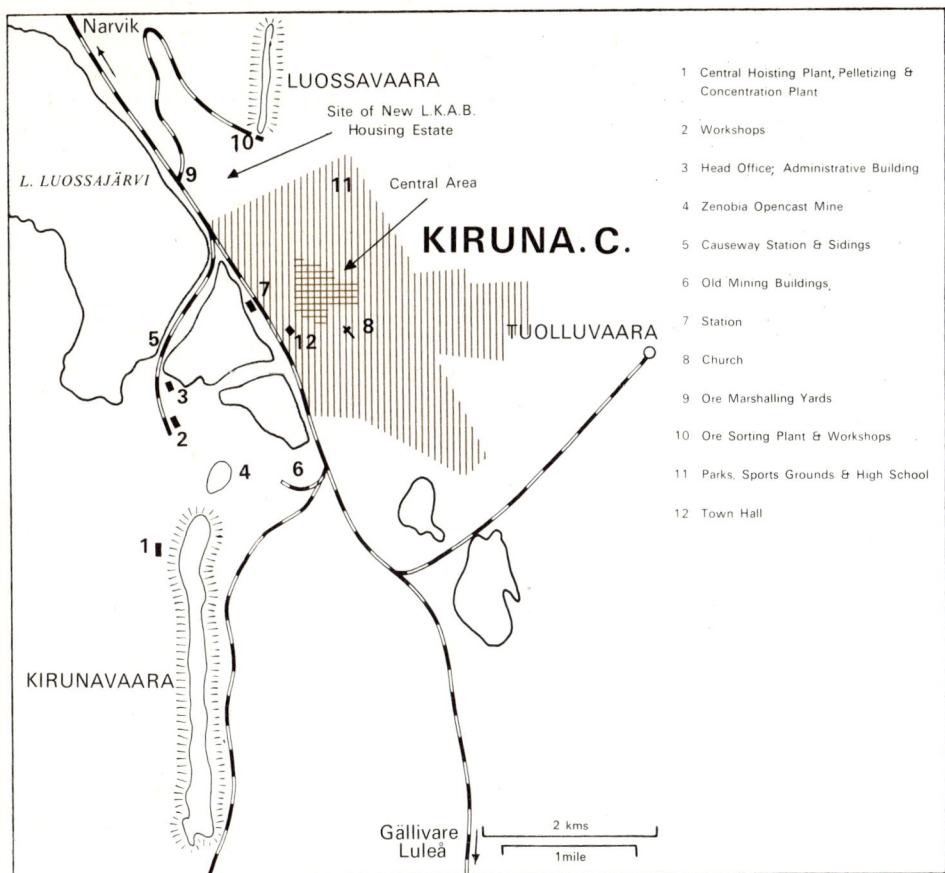

Figure 4. Sketch map of Kiruna.

centres of population in Sweden is to some extent reduced by the air services operating from the two aerodromes shown on the map extract (Kiruna Flygplats 7223, and Kalixfors Flygplats 6817).

However, life is not easy in Kiruna, especially in winter when there is a six weeks period of continuous darkness and temperatures may be as low as −40°C. Snow lingers in the streets until June. A combination of lack of sunlight in winter and the intense cold forces many people from the south to return to a more congenial climate after several years in the north.

A key factor in the development of Kiruna has been the abundant supply of cheap hydroelectric power from the ungraded, rejuvenated rivers of the region. The map shows numerous power lines converging on the town. These carry the essential power for the iron workings, the town and the railways.

The bulk of the electricity comes from the generating station at Porjus, some 60 miles (96 km) to the south of Kiruna, but this source is supplemented by smaller, local power stations along the Torneälv and Kalixälv.

Apart from Kiruna, the only nucleated settlement shown on the map extract is Tuolluvaara (population 1,400), which lies just to the north of the main road about 5 km from the centre of Kiruna. Otherwise the settlement is both scanty and dispersed. Isolated buildings are shown along the road south from Kiruna and by the shores of many of the lakes. The latter are linked to the roads by mere tracks and the map gives no indication of their function. It seems unlikely that they can be farms at such a high latitude, and they are more probably mountain huts belonging to the people of Kiruna. It is interesting to note that at 648176 there is a symbol denoting a Lapp camp. Such camps consist of a collection of tents and turf-huts (*Kåta*) occupied by reindeer-herding Lapps. About 800 reindeer-owning Lapps with over 30,000 animals are found in the Kiruna district.

Although life is hard in Kiruna it is also clear that the iron deposits constitute one of the great assets of Sweden. The continuing importance that is attached to these metal resources of the north is indicated by the opening in 1964 of a new mine at Svappavaara, approximately midway between Kiruna and Gällivare. This mine, which has the third largest output in Sweden after Kiruna and Malmberget, is already attracting settlement in a manner reminiscent of Kiruna at the beginning of the century.

The following terms which are of Finnish origin occur frequently on the map extract.
Jänkä Marsh; swamp *Joki* River; stream
Järvi Lake *Vaara* Mountain

Exercises

1. Explain the difference between isostatic and eustatic changes of base level. Describe the effect of such changes on the coastal and inland features of the Scandinavian Peninsula.
2. Make a comparison of the economic development of Arctic Norway and Arctic Sweden.
3. Explain precisely the meaning of the following terms which occur in the chapter: *(a)* polycyclic erosion; *(b)* monadnock; *(c)* porphyry; *(d)* permafrost; *(e)* gley soil.
4. Illustrate the statement that people will live in the most inhospitable areas provided that the incentives are sufficiently great. (O. & C.)
5. Describe the evolution and present character of two contrasting regions of iron ore production. (W.J.E.C.)

Further Reading

MEAD, W. R. *An Economic Geography of the Scandinavian States and Finland*, London U.P., 2nd Edition, 1968, chapter 12.
O'DELL, A. C. *The Scandinavian World*, Longmans, 1957, chapter 8.
SØMME, A., ed. *The Geography of Norden*. Heinemann, 1961, chapter 12.
WATTS, N. 'Kiruna. Sweden's northernmost mining town', *Geographical Magazine*, **38**, 1955.

Study 4
COPENHAGEN
DENMARK

Extract From Map Sheet 1513.
København.
Danish 1:100,000 Series.

Revised 1968.
Vertical interval of contours 5 metres.

By permission A.236/67 of the Geodetic Institute of Denmark.

Map 4

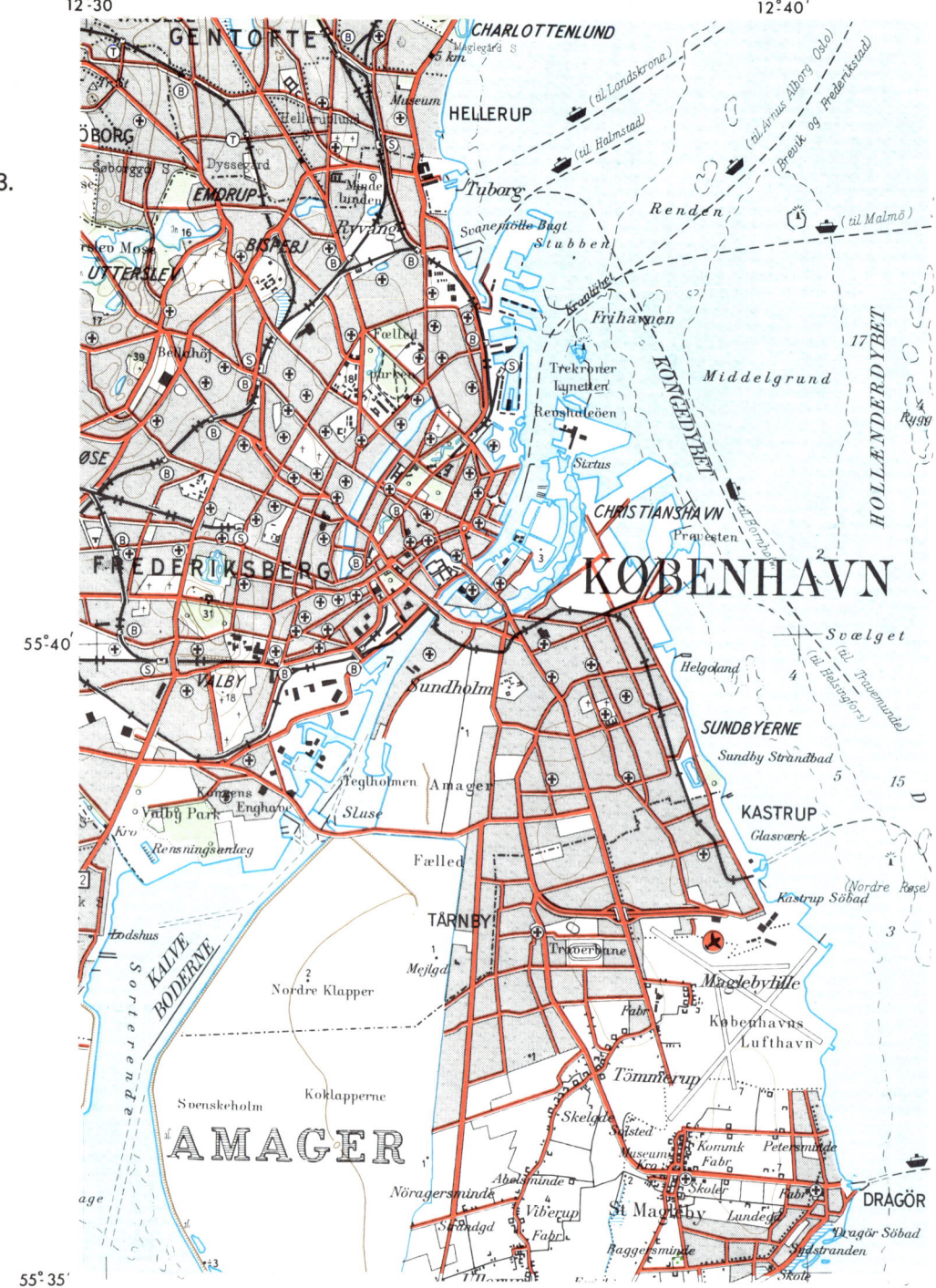

Six different maps series covering Denmark are available at scales ranging from 1:20,000 to 1:300,000. The map extract of Copenhagen is taken from one of the 1:100,000 sheets. The mapping of urban areas at such a scale presents many problems to the cartographer, on account of the over-abundance of detail of streets and buildings requiring presentation. Considerable elimination of features of the urban landscape and local place names is obviously inevitable in the interests of the legibility of the map sheet. However, the map extract gives a useful, if somewhat generalised, picture of the site and form of central Copenhagen.

Copenhagen plays a commanding role in the geography of Denmark. The 1965 statistics showed the three censal districts of Copenhagen, Fredericksberg and Gentofte to have populations of 681,717, 110,657 and 85,477 respectively, giving a total population of 877,851 for the city. If the population of the growing suburban districts is added to this figure, Greater Copenhagen has a population of about 1,400,000 out of a total population of 4,741,000 for the country as a whole. This concentration in the capital city of approximately 30% of the national population is unique in Europe (apart from Iceland, where as much as 70% of the population lives in Reykjavik) and, as in England with its drift of population to the south east, the rapid growth of the Danish metropolitan region is causing much concern.

Site and position

Copenhagen is situated on the eastern shore of Sjælland, the largest of the Danish islands, overlooking Öre Sund (The Sound), the deepest and most important of the three entrance channels to the Baltic. It also lies on the east-west route between Jylland and southern Sweden and has frequent ferry services to Landskrona and Malmö in Skåne. Its position may thus be regarded as a link between the North Sea and the Baltic and between Central Europe and the Scandinavian Peninsula. Its peripheral position in relation to the Danish territory is a result of historical circumstances, for until 1660 Denmark held control of what is now the Skåne region of Sweden. With the loss of this territory the position of Copenhagen was changed from that of a central city to a frontier city overlooking Swedish lands across Öre Sund.

The key factor in the siting of Copenhagen is the narrow strait running between the main island of Sjælland and the smaller island of Amager to the south-east (see photograph 4). From early times this provided a sheltered, deep-water anchorage for shipping. (A depth of 7 metres is indicated at one point in the channel.) The main access to this channel, which is protected by a system of locks *(Sluse)* to the south, is the narrow deep-water approach

Photograph 4. Copenhagen, showing the channel between Sjælland and Amager and details of the urban morphology of the inner town. In the foreground is the main city station with the Tivoli Gardens beyond. The large building in the centre of the picture is the Christiansborg Palace on the island of Slotsholm.

Luftfoto Nowico, Copenhagen.

of Kronlöbet to the north which links with the main shipping lanes of Öre Sund. Extensive modern additions to the natural harbour have been developed on reclaimed land at the northern end of the strait and even on a small scale on the open section of coast as at Tuborg, Kastrup and Dragör. Altogether Copenhagen possesses over 12,000 yards of developed water frontage, a figure far in excess of any other Scandinavian port.

The terrain on the northern side of the strait is gently undulating and reaches a maximum height of 39 metres in the Bellahöf district. The original drainage pattern has no doubt been much modified and diverted with the growth of the city, and in fact no surface streams are shown to reach the sea in this area. Factors of site appear to have imposed few limitations on the urban morphology to the north of the strait. This contrasts with Amager. The western part of the smaller island is extremely low lying and is in fact crossed by a sea-level contour. A spot height of 3 metres below sea-level is indicated at one point. The area is maintained only by a system of embankments, artificial drainage channels and constant pumping. The nature of the site in this instance imposes a complete control over the direction of urban expansion, although it is interesting to note how an extensive area of flat and previously undeveloped land along the eastern side of Amager has been utilised for Kastrup Airport. It is unusual for such a space-consuming land use to be located at a distance of less than six kilometres from a city centre as in the case of Copenhagen.

Historical development

The first record of Copenhagen (Kœpmanna Havn) dates from the 11th century when it was described as a fishing village and trading place. The settlement was fortified in 1167 and created a city in 1254. Following its development as a trading centre by the Hanseatic League, the potential advantages of its position were fully realised. After the break-up of the Hanse trading organisation Copenhagen continued to maintain its commercial importance, unlike many cities which flourished temporarily under the Hanse merchants. Shipping through Öre Sund brought continued prosperity during the 16th and 17th centuries, and it was not until the 19th century that Copenhagen abandoned the right to collect dues from all shipping passing between the Kattegat and Baltic. However, prior to the 17th century the city remained small and compact and was confined to the area between the strait and the lake (at present crossed by four bridges) to the west. During the 17th century the Christianshavn area, with its fortifications, at the northern end of Amager was developed. During the 18th and 19th centuries the built-up area was extended beyond the lake into the

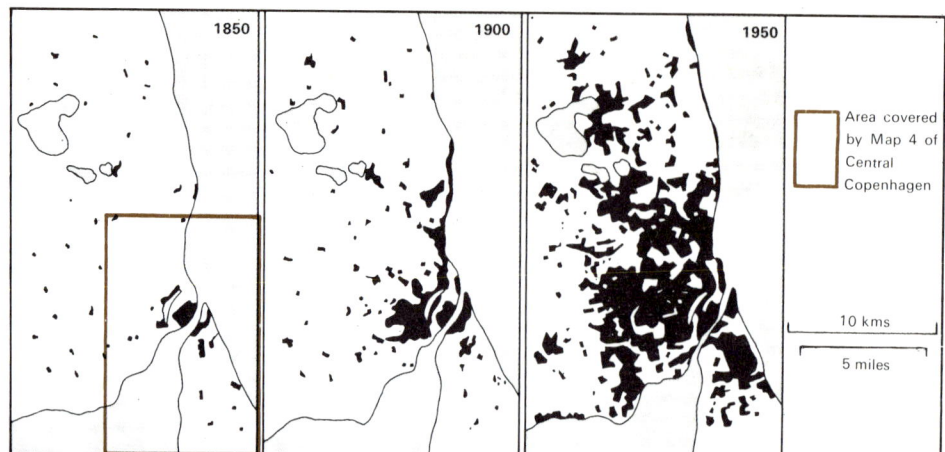

Figure 5. The growth of Copenhagen, 1850–1950 (after N. Nielsen.)

Frederiksberg district and the area around Fælled Park. The extent of the city by the end of the nineteenth century can be seen from figure 5 above. During the period 1850 to 1900 the city's population increased from 130,000 to 450,000.

The early decades of the 19th century marked a period of stagnation and decline in the development of the port. Recovery came with the late 19th century growth of a variety of modern industries including metal-working, engineering, shipbuilding, chemicals, textiles, clothing, printing, brewing and food industries. In 1894 the opening of the Kiel Canal, which provided a more direct means of entry into the Baltic than Öre Sund, was regarded as a major threat to the prosperity of Copenhagen and its traditional role at the entrance to the Baltic, and in order to counteract this development a Freeport (Frihavn) was created in the same year at the northern end of the harbour works. Copenhagen Freeport is now one of the great transit ports of Europe. The 7,644,000 tons of Danish imports entering through Copenhagen in 1964 included petroleum, coal, metal ores, timber, fertilizers and oil seeds. Exports in the same year amounted to 1,652,000 tons (these figures exclude transit trade).

During the early part of the present century the districts of Valby, Sundbyerne and Tårnby were incorporated into the city. More recent expansion has been concentrated in a westward and northward direction along road and rail routes out of the city, and many former villages have been swallowed up in the suburban spread at a rate which is exceptional in Scandinavia (fig. 5). Industrial expansion in Copenhagen has also been very striking during the post-war period. These newer industries include oil refining and the production of consumer goods, especially luxury products such as glassware, fine fabrics and furniture, which may be regarded as the modern equivalents of the city's traditional porcelain industry. At the present time more than 45% of Denmark's industrial workers are employed in Copenhagen.

Urban morphology

Although a map scale of 1:100,000 is really inadequate for examining city structures, certain broad observations may be made about the urban form in the part of central Copenhagen shown on the map extract. The original nucleus of the settlement lay on the tiny island of Slotsholm (to the immediate north of the present railway bridge across the strait). Early growth was in the area between the strait and the lake to the west. This is the present central area of the city and contains the oldest buildings in Copenhagen, many dating back to Denmark's medieval period of greatness. It is the principal shopping district of the city and also includes banks and commercial premises, the main entertainments, museums and university buildings. As can be seen from photograph 4 the density of building is extremely high in this area and the arrangement of the narrow streets lacks a clear plan.

The 19th century extensions which lie chiefly within the inner 'circle' of the railway system show a tendency towards a rectilinear layout, as can be seen in the distance on photograph 4. Harbour works with their associated warehouses and industrial premises lie chiefly at the northern end of the strait, and to a lesser extent in the vicinity of the docks to the south. Although certain of the larger factories are indicated on the map (*Fabrik* abb. *Fabr.* = a factory), industrial areas are difficult to locate, but in fact show a close relationship to the city's railway system as well as the port.

The small part of suburban Copenhagen that is shown on the extract appears to be well connected to the central area by a radial pattern of roads and railways. On Amager Island it appears that the village of St. Magleby is becoming incorporated into the urban fabric by the same process that has transformed the former villages of Tårnby and Dragör into city suburbs. Several beaches (*Strand*) and bathing places (*Söbad*) are marked along the outer coast of Amager, suggesting that the island may be an important summer recreational area for the city.

The Copenhagen region is the area of most striking urban growth in Scandinavia and is in many ways unique in the geography of northern Europe. In fact both shores of Öre Sund are attracting industry and settlement to such an extent as to prompt the remark that 'Copenhagen, the capital of Denmark's former Scandinavian empire and northern Europe's largest city, promises to become the centre of the first conurbation in Scandinavia' (R. Millward).

Exercises

1. With reference to an atlas, draw a sketch map to show the position of Copenhagen in relation to southern Scandinavia. Show the chief towns, railways and ferry links in the region.
2. Illustrate the disadvantages that may result from towns becoming too large. (O. & C.)
3. What was the Hanseatic League? Draw a map to show the towns and cities that belonged to the Hanseatic organisation. Examine the present day importance of these towns and relate their relative rates of growth or decline to the factor of geographical position.
4. Explain precisely what is meant by the term 'Freeport'. With reference to examples from western Europe, examine the conditions under which their creation has been necessary.
5. With reference to the map extract and the text, construct a map to show the main aspects of the historical growth and present functional areas within the city. Your map should show the extent of the city at different periods together with the present central business district, residential districts, industrial areas, harbour works, open spaces, land unsuitable for building, etc.
6. In such a fragmented country as Denmark, ferry services constitute vital links in the communications system. The following table gives ferry sailings from Copenhagen. Construct a flowline diagram to show the intensity of traffic along the various routes.

Copenhagen to:	Sailings per week	Copenhagen to:	Sailings per week
Aalborg	14	Horsens	3
Aarhus	14	Kolding	2
Allinge (Bornholm)	6	Landskrona (Sweden)	80
Ballen (Samsø)	2	Malmö (Sweden)	80
Fredericia	2	Neksö (Bornholm)	6
Frederikshavn	2	Odense (Fyn)	2
Grenaa	1	Randers	3
Gudheim (Bornholm)	6	Rønne (Bornholm)	7
Hasle (Bornholm)	6	Svaneke (Bornholm)	4
		Vejle	3

(Based on time-tables for Summer 1966. Unless specified, the ferry ports are on the coast of East Jylland.)

Further reading

Denmark. The Royal Danish Ministry of Foreign Affairs and the Danish Statistical Department, Copenhagen, 1961.
EAST, W. G. *An Historical Geography of Europe*, 4th edn, Methuen 1950, chapter 16.
MILLWARD, R. *Scandinavian Lands*, Macmillan, 1964, chapter 4.
MORGAN, F. W. and BIRD, J. *Ports and Harbours*, 2nd edn, Hutchinson, 1958.
NIELSEN, N. and AAGESEN, A. 'Greater Copenhagen. An urbanised area and its geographical growth', 'The Copenhagen district and its population', both in *Guide Book to Denmark*, ed. Niels Jacobsen, Copenhagen University Geographical Institute on the occasion of the International Geographical Congress Norden 1960.
SØMME, A., ed. *The Geography of Norden*, Heinemann, 1961, chapter 8.
Denmark. Naval Intelligence Geographical Handbook Series, 1944.

Study 5
GEESTMERAM-BACHT POLDER NORTH HOLLAND NETHERLANDS

A Polder Landscape.

Extract from Map Sheets
19 West Alkmaar and
14 West Medemblik.
Dutch 1:50,000 Series.

Revised 1959.

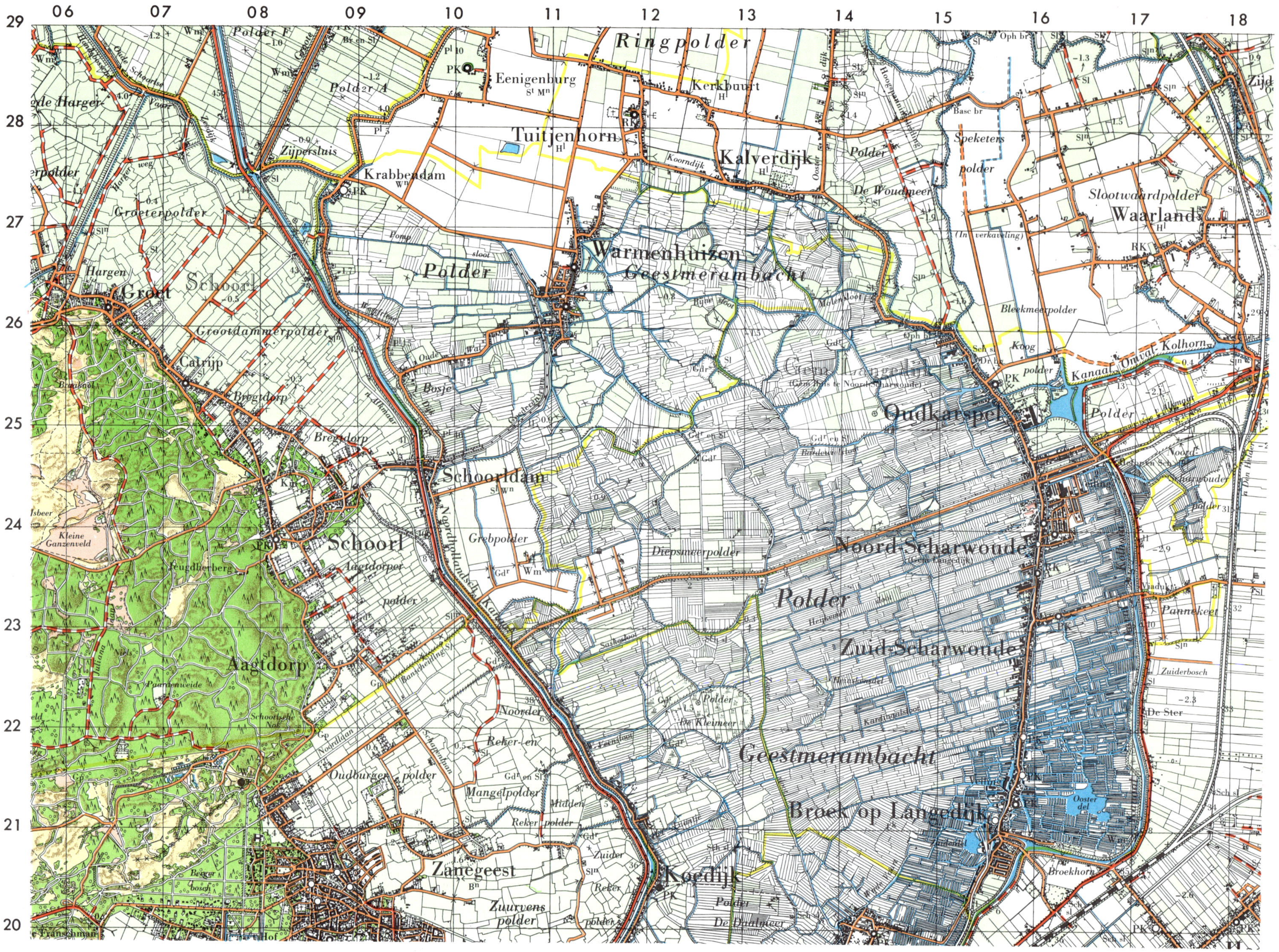

By permission of Topografische Dienst, Delft, Netherlands.

Map 5

Photograph 5. View across the Geestmerambacht Polder towards the North Sea.

KLM Aerocarto, Amsterdam.

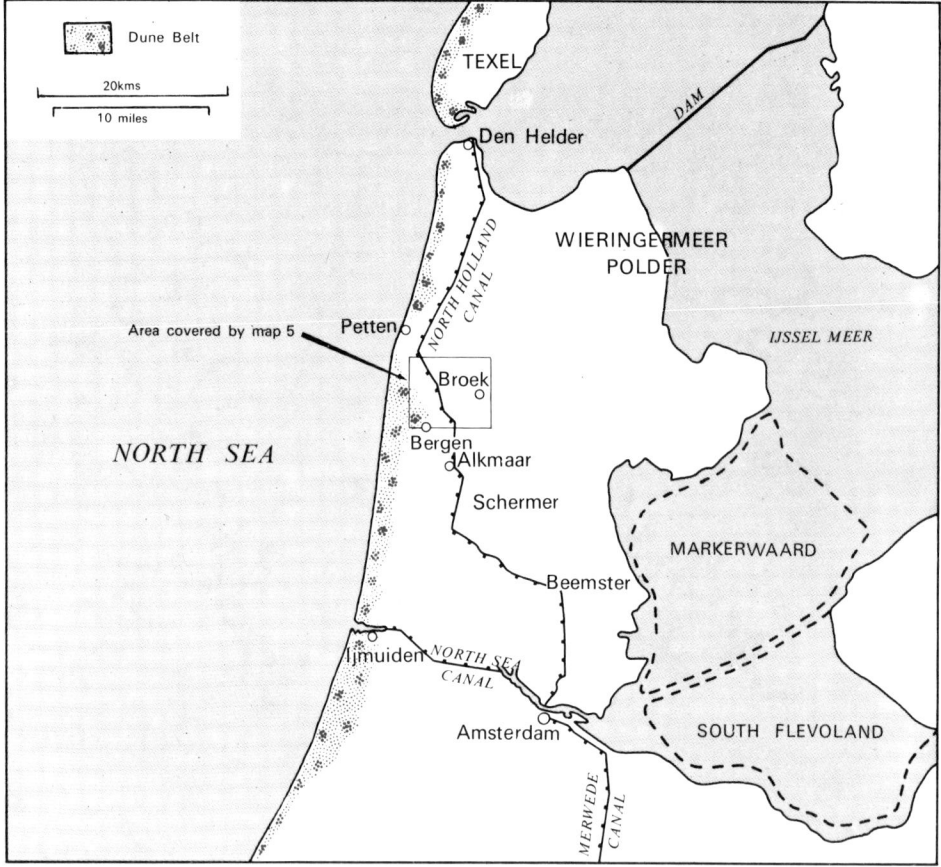

Figure 6. North Holland.

The following study is based upon extracts from the 1:25,000 and 1:50,000 maps of the Netherlands. Relief is shown by contours at 5 metre intervals on the 1:50,000 map and at 2·5 metre intervals on the 1:25,000 series. Additional information is provided by spot heights. One of the most useful features of both maps is the attention given to land use. Distinctions are made between arable and pastoral land, glasshouses and orchards, as well as between various types of woodland and heath. This presents the geographer with information that is unobtainable from the topographical maps of most other countries.

The landscape shown on photograph 5 and on maps 5 and 6 is without doubt one of the most artificial or manmade in Europe. The area is a Dutch polder landscape in the province of North Holland which lies between the North Sea in the west and the former Zuider Zee in the east. Some 4 km to the south of the map extract lies Alkmaar, an important centre for much of North Holland.

Landscape

In the south-west corner of map extract 5 lies an area of dune country. Although no spot heights are to be seen on this part of the map, the area does in fact reach heights well above sea level. (A height of 30 metres is attained at a point about 1 km west of the extract.) In this section the dune belt is comparatively wide, but further north (vide top centre and right of photograph 5) the line of dunes is much narrower and is, in fact, non-existent in the vicinity of Petten, in the top left of the photograph. The dune belt is Holland's great defence against the encroachment of the North Sea. It extends, with minor breaks as at Petten where an artificial bank has been constructed, from the Hook of Holland to Den Helder. Beyond Den Helder the line of dunes is discontinuous and forms the West Frisian Islands. The dunes are of relatively recent formation, dating from after the end of the Quaternary Ice Age at about the time of the breaching of the Straits of Dover (*c.* 5000 B.C.). A great offshore bar was developed by wave action, continuous, except for the mouths of the Maas and Rhine, from western Flanders to northern Germany. Upon this bar windblown sand accumulated as dunes. Behind the dune belt shallow lagoons became regions of accumulation for mud, and later plants and beds of peat. The largest of these lagoons was Lake Flevo. Subsequent invasions by the sea during historic times, and especially in the 14th century, transformed these fresh-water lagoons into salt-water areas, Lake Flevo, for example, forming the even larger Zuider Zee. Gulfs of the Zuider Zee extended westwards at this time almost to the dune rampart, notably in the Beemster and Schermer areas adjacent to Alkmaar. The polder lands of the Netherlands are the result of man's efforts to drain these low-lying regions of peat, silt and clay.

The greater part of the landscape shown on map extract 5 and photograph 5 is polder land. Examination of both maps will show the height of the floors of the polders to be well below sea level. Only in the south west, on the land between the North Holland Canal and the dune belt, are heights above sea level recorded.

The method of reclamation of the polder lands consisted of the construction of a long dyke, on the outside of which lay a peripheral canal known as a *ring-vaart*. The area within the ring-dyke was pumped clear of water and a close, rectilinear pattern of drainage canals (*'Sloot' pl. 'Sloten'*) was established on the polder floor. Today, these are pumped into the *ring-vaart* which in turn is drained to other canals or rivers and eventually to the sea. Pumping is, of course, necessary because of the differences of levels which have been exaggerated in many areas by the shrinkage of the peat consequent upon drainage. (A similar problem is experienced in our own Fenland area.) Originally pumps were operated by wind, and the traditional Dutch windmill is still to be seen. However, in the 19th century, steam pumps, and more recently diesel and electric pumps, have largely superseded the older method.

In areas where the floors of the polders are above mean sea level the problem of drainage is easier, since less pumping needs to be done. Such an area is to be found in the south-west of extract 5 as, for example, in Mangel polder, Oudburger polder and Zuurvens polder.

The greater part of the map extracts are covered by the Geestmerambacht Polder, which stretches from the North Holland Canal in the west to the canal running from 153290 to 153200 in the east. Within the main polder there are some fourteen separate smaller polders which are drained into the main canals. These in turn are drained to the Schermerboezem, which acts as a water storage area and lies to the south of Alkmaar. The most striking feature of the Geestmerambacht Polder is the very large area covered by water. Over the whole polder (5,660 hectares) about 20% is water-covered, and in the parish of Langedijk the figure is as high as 35%. The explanation is to be found in the history of the polder. Drained at an early date (14th century), the polder was important for vegetable cultivation even as early as the 16th century. Plots were improved by raising their levels with material dug out of the drainage channels. The dredged mud raised the plots, thereby securing better drainage together with improved fertility. The number and navigability of the ditches was also increased by the same process, which continued into the 20th century in response to urbanization in the Netherlands and the growing demand for fresh vegetables.

Land use

Although farming varies from arable to pastoral (the differences in colouring on the map being borne out by comparison with differences of tone on the photograph), the dominant impression is one of intensive land use. This is understandable when the high costs of drainage and maintenance are considered. The size of the plots varies considerably; the almost minute plots of the eastern part of the Geestmerambacht Polder contrast with those in the region around Waarland in the north-east of the map area and indeed with much of the rest of Holland.

A large part of the Geestmerambacht Polder is given over to horticulture, though in contrast to the Westland district between the Hague and the New Waterway most of the cultivation is carried out on open ground rather than under glass. In the Langedijk area green vegetables and early potatoes are an important interest, as the following table shows.

Horticultural crops on the Geestmerambacht Polder: 1961
(Expressed as percentages of the total horticultural area)

Parish	Green vegetables on open ground	Early potatoes	Bulbs	Onions	Remainder
Koedijk	64	29	5	1	1
Langedijk	57	32	7	3	1
St Pancras	50	36	12	1	1
Warmenhuizen	64	26	7	2	1
Polder as a whole	59	31	7	2	1

(*Note*: The parish of St Pancras is the most southerly of the parishes. The northern part of the village is shown at 1420.)

Source for all tables: Report for the Land Development Project for Geestmerambacht, Utrecht 1964.

The farms which concentrate on horticultural work are usually small. Moreover, the farm area tends to be split into numerous small plots.

Parish	Average no of plots per farm	Average size of plot in hectares
Koedijk	7.0	0.42
Langedijk	5.5	0.42
St Pancras	4.2	0.82
Warmenhuizen	4.0	1.03
Average	5.7	0.56

Farm sizes in Geestmerambacht Polder

Size of farm in hectares	Number of farms	
0–0.5	6	
0.5–1	23	
1–2	161	
2–3	205	
3–5	187	
5–7	40	Total
7–10	17	646
over 10	7	farms

The dominant farm size is between 1 and 5 hectares, which is not uneconomic for this type of cultivation. However, fragmentation into minute parcels of land causes difficulty. Reference to the map extract brings out very clearly the extremely small size of many of the Geestmerambacht plots compared with the more economic size of fields in the Heerhugowaard Polder which lies to the east and south.

Farms of a pastoral or arable nature producing crops such as sugar beet and wheat are much larger. In 1959 the total area occupied by the 134 farms of this type on the Geestmerambacht Polder was 1,400 hectares, which gives an average size per farm of 10.4 hectares. It is apparent from the maps that most of these farms lie in the north and west of the polder.

Much of the land west of the North Holland Canal and outside the Geestmerambacht Polder is devoted to permanent meadow or pasture. The emphasis in these areas is on dairying, with products such as cheese and

BROEK OP LANGEDIJK GEESTMERAMBACHT POLDER NORTH HOLLAND NETHERLANDS

Extract from Map Sheet 19B Alkmaar. Dutch 1:25,000 Series.

Revised 1959.

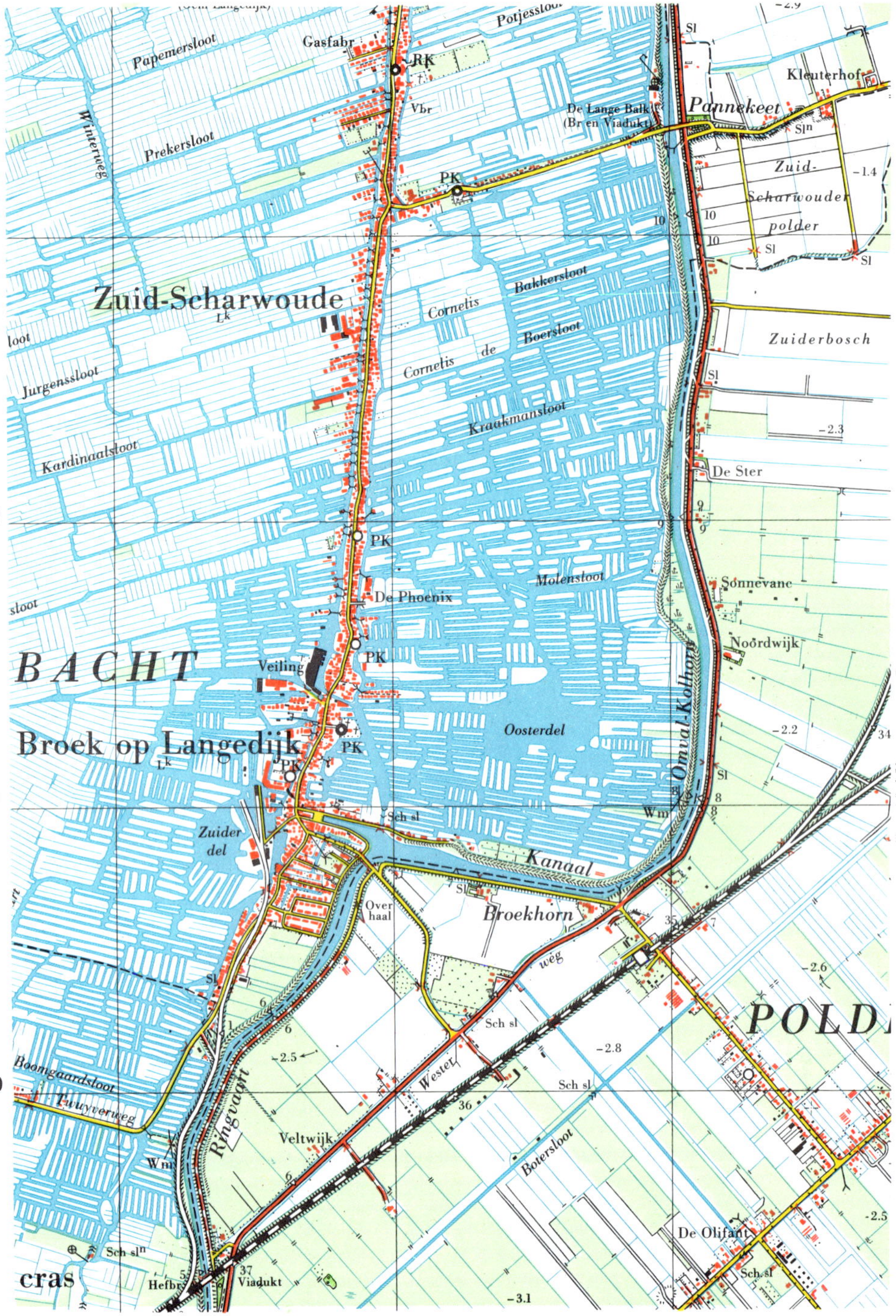

By permission of Topografische Dienst, Delft, Netherlands.

34 Map 6

Photograph 6. Broek op Langedijk. Note the style of the houses in the village and the "Veiling" or auction market in the foreground. Transport by boat plays an important part in farming in this area.
KLM Aerocarto, Amsterdam.

butter for both home and export markets and fresh milk for nearby towns. Alkmaar, of course, is noted for its cheese market.

The only area not used for farmland lies in the south-west. Even here some return may be obtained from the pine trees, although they were originally planted with a view to stabilising the dunes.

Settlement and communications

The settlements in the area fall into two groups; those on the polders and those at the foot of the dunes. On the polder land villages are confined to higher ground along the roads which border the canals. Thus, most settlements in these areas are of a 'street-village' type, consisting of one road with little depth of housing either side. Comparison of maps and photograph will give the names of several of these linear settlements, although perhaps the most striking is Scharwoude (Nord and Zuid) which is continuous with Oudkarspel and Broek op Langedijk over a distance of more than 6 km.

On the Geestmerambacht Polder it is remarkable how dwellings are concentrated in the villages and not dispersed throughout the farmlands. The evidence of the map is confirmed by the following figures.

Population figures (1962) for the parishes of Geestmerambacht Polder

Parish	Total population	Villages	Population	% in village
Langedijk	9,278	Broek	2,500	
		Zuid Scharwoude	1,500	
		Nöord Scharwoude	3,200 } 8,900	
		Oudkarspel	1,700	96
St Pancras	1,728	St Pancras	1,600	93
Warmenhuizen	2,757	Warmenhuizen	2,200	80
Koedijk	2,338	Koedijk	1,100	47

The comparatively low figure of 47% for Koedijk is accounted for by the extension of the settlement alongside the road above the North Holland Canal, and by a separate nucleation south of the village of St Pancras.

On the higher land at the foot of the dune belt the control exerted by minor relief is not so close, and most villages, together with the town of Bergen (0820), show a less linear pattern. However, the road following the foot of the dunes from Groet (0626) is bordered by dwellings throughout most of its length. Settlement is more dispersed in this region, although the popular sites lie in a belt at the junction of the dunes and farmlands.

As with settlements, communications are similarly affected by minor variations in height. The road system is obviously of great importance in a region producing crops for both urban and export markets. Roads often follow the lines of the higher drainage canals, although some are built on embankments separate from those of the waterways. The roads are mostly of a good standard, and only in the west is there evidence of unmetalled or loose-surfaced roads. Railways are of less significance, with one single-track line in the east which improves to double-track status before it leaves the map area in the south. Canals are of great importance for moving bulky produce such as sugar beet, fertilisers and building materials. The largest is the North Holland Canal, which follows a north-north-west to south-south-east course across the area linking Amsterdam with Den Helder in the north.

Problems of the region

The Geestmerambacht Polder is one of the economic problem areas of the Dutch polder lands. Certain points are suggested by a close study of the map and a consideration of the figures given earlier:

(a) The remarkable absence of roads in all but the most northerly parts of the Geestmerambacht Polder.

(b) The minute size of most plots of land in the area.

(c) The fragmented nature of the holdings on the Polder. As in other parts of Europe this is partly the result of the piecemeal purchase of land.

In earlier times it was of little significance if vegetable produce was conveyed by small boats and grown on very small plots. Wages were low and labour abundant for tilling the soil, transporting the produce and maintaining the intricate system of waterways. Today the position is different. With high labour costs, mechanisation becomes necessary if the farming of these areas is to be reasonably profitable. Similarly the maintenance of countless waterways and the slow and expensive transportation of produce by small boats is quite out of keeping with modern needs. The Land Reclamation Project for Geestmerambacht Polder was published in 1964 and was an attempt to find answers to these problems. It envisages the enlargement and consolidation of land holdings into more viable units and the establishment of a much denser road network; that is to say, a replacement of waterway polders by a series of roadway polders similar to those in the north-east near Waarland (1727). Accompanying the plans for consolidation of land holdings will come a rebuilding programme for dwelling and farm houses. These will be sited close to the farmland and should result in a more dispersed pattern of settlement than at present exists on Geestmerambacht Polder. Reclamation work started in 1967, but such is the scale of work involved that completion is not expected until 1976.

Exercises

1. Identify the following features shown by letters on photograph 5:
(a) the water area marked A; *(b)* the building B; *(c)* the cluster of buildings at C; *(d)* the villages at D, E and F.

By comparing photograph 5 with the two map extracts, find *(a)* the direction and angle of view of the photograph; *(b)* the approximate observation point of the photograph.

2. Compare and contrast the landscape, land use, settlement and communication patterns of the area east of easting 15 and north of northing 26 with the Geestmerambacht Polder between the North Holland Canal and the Omval-Kolhorn Canal and south of the road from Oudkarspel to 106228.

3. What further useful information can be gained by studying the 1:25,000 map extract in addition to the 1:50,000?

4. Agricultural patterns in advanced countries are more affected by cultural, economic and political factors than by purely physical factors. Discuss.

Further reading

GRAFTDIJK, K. *Holland Rides the Sea,* World's Window Ltd, Baarn, Holland. 1964.
LAMBERT, A. 'Farm consolidation and improvement in the Netherlands', *Economic Geography* 37, 1961.
MONKHOUSE, F. J. *The Countries of North-western Europe,* Longmans, 1965, chapter 8.
MONKHOUSE, F. J., *A Regional Geography of Western Europe,* Longmans, 1965, chapter 3.
Netherlands, Naval Intelligence Geographical Handbook Series, 1944.
WAGRET, P. *Polderlands,* Methuen, 1968.

Study 6
LIÈGE
BELGIUM

An Old Industrial District

Belgium produces a variety of topographical maps at scales ranging from 1:15,000 to 1:200,000. The chosen extract is from the 1:50,000 series (Type R) which is characterised by a very bold cartographic style and the inclusion of a great wealth of detail.

The position of Liège

Liège, the fourth city of Belgium, has a population of 156,000 and forms the centre of a conurbation with a population of over 500,000. It stands at the eastern end of the Sambre-Meuse Depression where the river Meuse is joined by the rivers Ourthe and Vesdre, which are unnamed on the map extract but enter the area from the south and south-east respectively. The Liège district forms the eastern end of the Franco-Belgian coalfield which stretches in a great crescent some 140 miles long from Pas-de-Calais in France through Charleroi and Namur to the area shown on the map extract. To the north of Liège lies the relatively recently developed Campine (Kempen) coalfield.

The valley of the Meuse between Namur and Liège, together with that of its tributary the river Sambre, follows the axis of a synclinorium exposed by the erosion and removal of a former cover of overlying rocks. South of Namur the Meuse valley runs discordantly across a series of fold structures and has not adjusted its course to the present cover of rocks. This is usually interpreted as an example of superimposed drainage. To the south of the deeply incised Sambre-Meuse valley lies a dissected plateau known in the west as Entre-Sambre-et-Meuse and in the east as the Condroz. The map extract includes part of the northern edge of the Condroz which, on account of its similarities with the main Ardenne Plateau to the south, is known locally as the Ardenne Condrusienne.

Examination of an atlas map will reveal the importance of the position and alignment of the Sambre-Meuse Depression. The navigable river and its valley provide a natural route between two of the most densely populated and heavily industrialised regions in western Europe, namely northern France and the Ruhr, while just below Liège the Albert Canal leads from the Meuse across the Campine region to Antwerp.

Relief and drainage of the Liège district

Although very complex in detail, the area may be described in general terms as a dissected plateau cut across by the deep, steep-sided valley of the river Meuse. As T. H. Elkins remarks in describing the area, 'Everywhere the plateaux dominate, their even summits barring the horizon'. The land is highest and the plateau surface best preserved to the south of the river where resistant sandstones of Lower Devonian age outcrop at the surface. Maximum heights of over 240 metres are encountered to the south-west of Ougrée where there is a marked flattening of the hill summits. The edge of the high, heavily wooded ground between the Ourthe and Meuse is dissected by deep, narrow valleys occupied by small streams such as the Villencourt and Lize. Several of these streams are intermittent in character and none appear to reach the main river. It is impossible to say from the map evidence whether this is a result of the local geology or a lowering of the water table by excessive pumping or the diversion of the streams into underground conduits. Where the edge of the high ground is not dissected by tributary valleys the bordering slopes are extremely steep, with gradients in excess of 1 in 3 as, for example, between Ougrée and Angleur. This wooded cliff overlooking the Meuse is in fact a faultline escarpment related to the Eifel Fault which runs from the vicinity of Val-St-Lambert through the southern suburbs of Seraing and Ougrée towards Angleur.

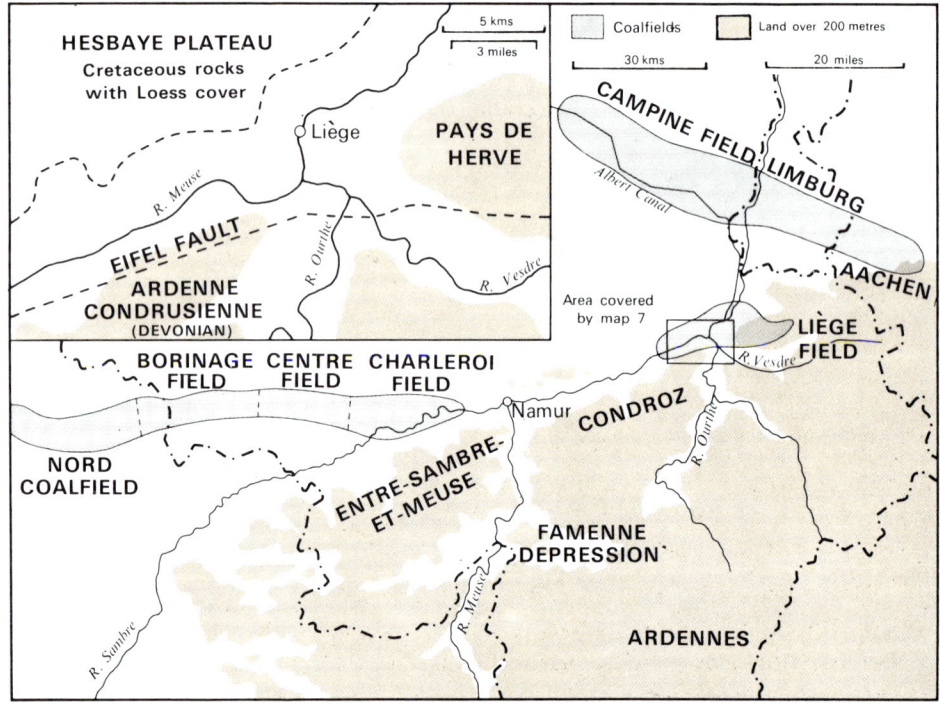

Figure 7. The coalfields of Belgium and neighbouring areas.

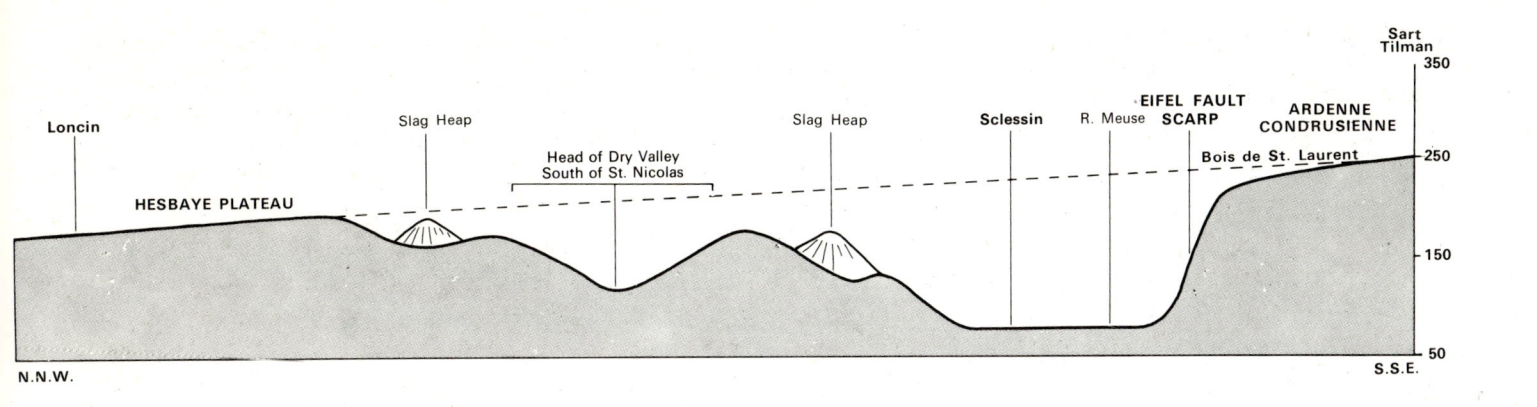

Figure 8. Section across the Meuse valley. Cross-section from Sart Tilman (South-east of Ougrée) to Loncin (North-west of Liège). Horizontal scale 1:50,000. Vertical scale 1":200 metres. Notice the continuation of the surface of the Ardenne Condrusienne across the Meuse valley onto the Hesbaye Plateau which declines northwards.

The western side of the assymetrical Ourthe valley is similarly steep with cliff-like slopes where the meanders abut the valley sides. The relief of the area to the east of the Ourthe is less striking and rises more gently to heights of over 200 metres. This is the edge of the Pays De Herve, another plateau surface with dry valleys and intermittent streams.

To the north of the river Meuse the ground again rises steeply on to the Hesbaye Plateau, a dissected surface of Cretaceous rocks with a loess cover. Reference to photograph 7 shows that apart from the various slag heaps the skyline of this area is strikingly flat and even. The highest ground here is found in the vicinity of Montegnée where heights of over 190 metres are reached. A large branching valley runs from Hollogne-aux-Pierres to join the main valley at Jemeppe, while similar dry valleys penetrate the high ground from Tilleur and Liège. As is true of the map area as a whole, the district north of the Meuse is characterised by a general lack of surface drainage. Several wells are shown in the extreme north of the area and the large number of water towers indicates the need for storage of water to meet the needs of the large urban population.

The river Meuse meanders across the area in a deep, trench-like valley and has incised itself some 140 metres below the bordering uplands. The river is not shown to cross any contours on the map and it may therefore be deduced that its fall is very slight. The valley floor varies considerably in width but is very flat, and stands at a height of just under 80 metres. Liège and Seraing both stand at points where the valley floor is wider than elsewhere, and where, in the case of Liège, there is a notable embayment of low ground on the north bank of the river. Photograph 7, which is taken from the slopes above Ougrée, shows the flat ground bordering the river in the vicinity of Sclessin.

Mining and industry

Although the key for the Belgium 1:50,000 map series gives the abbreviation 'Charb' (Charbonnage) for coalmines, this does not appear on the map extract, and one must rely on the distribution of spoil heaps which are marked by hachures to obtain a picture of the location of coal-mining activity. Of course the number of such slag heaps may not correlate exactly with the actual number of collieries, since a single colliery may dispose of waste material at more than one point, and there is no means of determining how many of these spoil banks, the product of more than 150 years large scale commercial exploitation of the coal, are related to disused mines. For example, between 1957 and 1965 the number of woking pits on the Sambre-Meuse coalfield fell by 59% from 113 to 47. However, it is clear that the coalfield occupies a much broader belt of ground on the northern side of the river than on the southern side. Over 30 slag heaps are shown on the Hesbaye Plateau compared with only about 7 to the south. The southern limit of mining is determined by the Eifel Fault which marks the junction between the Lower Devonian rocks of the Ardenne Condrusienne and the coal measures to the north (fig. 7).

As in other coalfield districts of the Sambre-Meuse Depression, mining in the Liège area is both difficult and expensive on account of the arrangement of the coal seams. The coal measures, lying along the margin of the Ardennes, were greatly affected by the Hercynian orogeny and are intensively folded and faulted. F. J. Monkhouse quotes an example near Mons where, as a result of faulting and overthrusting 'a single shaft 1,115 feet in depth passes through the same seam six times'. Furthermore the most easily mined seams have long been worked out. The Liège coalfield in fact has the lowest productivity of all the Belgian coalfields, and compares unfavourably with

LIÈGE
BELGIUM

Published 1963.
Map revised from aerial photographs 1947. Last complete field revision 1931-35. Rapid field revision 1953. Roads up-to-date 1963.
Vertical interval of contours 10 metres.

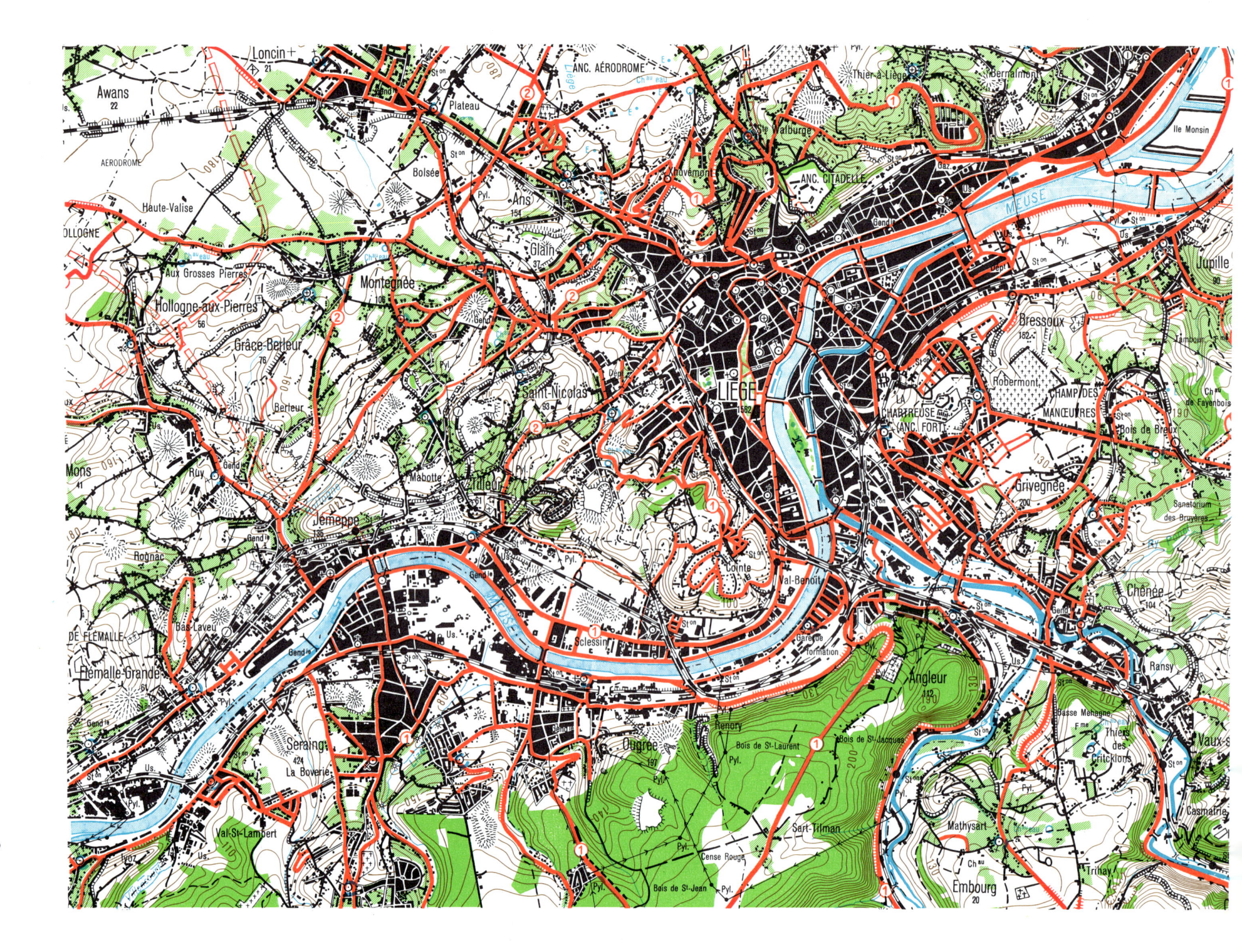

Extract from the 1:50,000 R map of Belgium—sheet of Liège.

Map 7

Photograph 7. The Meuse valley. View looking north-west across the Meuse valley from the slopes above Ougrée. Notice the crowding of factories and obsolete 19th century housing on the flat valley floor. In the distance is the edge of the Hesbaye Plateau with the tip-heaps from numerous collieries.

Cliché C.G.T.

the Campine coalfield to the north (see Exercise 6).

'Viewed against the wider European background, the position is more serious still. Belgium as a whole, even including the Campine, is, with its high wages and social security costs, a high cost producer, with a productivity per worker well below that of its neighbours in the European Coal and Steel Community. There is no doubt that in so far as the prosperity of Liège rests upon local coal it has an insecure foundation, and the difficulties of the industry will inevitably increase as the liberalizing measures of the Community expose it to foreign competition' (T. H. Elkins).

Fortunately the economy of Liège is based as much upon manufacturing as extractive industry. In 1964, 78,508 workers in the Liège district were employed in engineering and metal working trades compared with 18,341 in mining. However, the interpretation of the industrial geography of the Liège district from the map extract is very difficult. Large industrial premises are shown in the same manner as a street block in a densely built-up area, and little or no information is given about the type of industry present. Where symbols are used to denote particular industrial premises they are largely irrelevant to the contemporary industrial scene; thus the map provides a conventional sign for water mills, as along the Lize and Villencourt valleys, but has no special symbol to denote the huge complex of iron and steel works that lie along the Meuse at Seraing and Ougrée. The abbreviation *'Us' (Usine)* is shown in the key to indicate factory premises, but only a random selection appears to have been given this notation. A further guide to the industrial distribution in the area is provided by the small unshaded circles on the map, which denote large factory chimneys.

Industry in the Liège district is dominated by metal working, which was originally based on local iron ore, charcoal from the Condroz and water power from streams such as the Lize and Villencourt which join the Meuse from the bordering plateaux. At the present time the industry relies on coking coal from the Campine and Ruhr and imports of iron ore from Sweden, Luxembourg, France, Liberia, Mauritania, Brazil, etc. The origins of the modern, large-scale organisation of the iron and steel industry in the area date back to 1823, when the first Belgian blast furnace to use coke was established at Seraing by an English mechanic, John Cockerill. The industry is still centred at Seraing, and coking plants, blast furnaces, steel works and rolling mills all occupy the valley floor in the great bend of the Meuse at this point. Chemical works, using the by-products of the coking process, power stations and collieries also compete for the limited space along the banks of the waterway. At present most of the steel is produced by a small number of large integrated works. Two of the largest firms in the Liège district, 'S. A. John Cockerill' and 'S. A. Ougrée-Marinaye' merged in 1955 to form an enormous combine 'S. A. Cockerill-Ougrée', producing about a third of Belgium's annual output of steel. Also occupying premises on both banks of the river at Jemeppe and Seraing is another of the largest iron and steel concerns in Belgium, 'S. A. Métallurgique d'Espérance-Longdoz'. These foundries and works extend east from Seraing along both banks of the river through Ougrée and Sclessin to the southern districts of Liège. Engineering industries are found in the eastern suburbs, but the main function of the city is in the organisation of commerce rather than actual industrial production. Two other important industries in the area covered by the map extract are zinc smelting, along the Ourthe and Vesdre valleys, and the manufacture of plate glass at Val-St-Lambert in the south-west.

Settlement and communications

Probably the most striking feature about the map extract is the intensive spread of settlement and the close network of communications over almost the whole area. In addition to the main urban centres, where a 'completely built up area' is indicated by solid black shading, there are extensive districts where the amount and intensity of building is lesser only in degree. In fact a whole range of settlement types may be noted. Liège (population 156,000) stands alone in size and importance, the next largest towns being far smaller; namely Seraing (42,400), Grivegnée (20,000) and Bressoux (15,200) which are really suburbs of Liège, Ougrée (19,700), Jemeppe (13,500) and Angleur (11,200). On the Hesbaye Plateau a number of even smaller nucleated settlements may be noted including Montegnée (10,600), Tilleur (6,100) and Loncin (2,100). The figure alongside the various town names on the map is the 1954 population total in hundreds. In addition to the nucleated settlements which are linked by ribbon development along the main roads, there are many districts where a more dispersed pattern of settlement is evident, as for example in the area around St Nicholas west of Liège. Many of these areas are probably housing districts similar to the *cités ouvrières* of northern France. In other instances the map gives a suggestion of the incorporation of former villages into the general urban sprawl. In this district, as in many parts of Belgium, the distinction between urban and rural settlement is difficult to define. The general impression is one of unplanned, piecemeal development of housing associated with the local mining and industry. The lack of planning is particularly evident on the valley floor where residential areas lie interspersed with industrial premises.

Liège, of course, represents a different type of urban development. The original site of the city lay on the left bank slopes overlooking the flat valley floor. The Meuse formerly had a braided channel at this point, and the medieval expansion led to the occupance of a series of small islands between the various river channels. During the 18th and 19th centuries many of these shallow channels were infilled to form a number of wide boulevards through the central city. For example, the former Sauvenière meander of the river, enclosing the 'Quartier de l'Île', now forms a wide boulevard flanked by open spaces. The line of this route through the city centre on the left bank of the river is evident from the map, but a larger scale is required to reveal other correlations between the present street plan and the former channels of the river. At the present time Liège may be described as a compact settlement, confined by its valley site and with only limited extensions on to bordering plateaux.

Reference has been made to the position of Liège which occupies an important nodal position in the communications system of western Europe. On the map extract the broad pattern of valley and plateau routes which intersect in the area is obscured by the complexity and intensity of the local communications. Minor relief features, particularly the dry valleys, appear to exercise considerable control over the local road and rail pattern. Certain of the roads out of Liège are followed by tramways which suggest commuting from the outlying centres. The Albert Canal, which was opened in 1940, can be seen to branch off from the Meuse just below Liège. This allows vessels of up to 2,000 tons to reach the small port of Ile Monsin, but above Liège navigation is limited to vessels of a maximum of 600 tons capacity.

The Liège district presents the characteristic appearance and typical problems of 'old-established' areas of heavy industry on the coalfields of Europe. The industry of the area is an example of geographical inertia and is, in many respects, ill adapted to modern conditions and finds difficulty in competing with more recently established industries elsewhere. The obsolete nature of much of the building on the valley floor is apparent from the photograph, and, as F. J. Monkhouse points out, 'it is obvious that much of the southern coalfield is an 'old' industrial area from its appearance. Derelict collieries, overgrown spoil banks, a chaos of pit-shafts, blast-furnaces and steel-works, chemical factories, long rows of small, drab, gardenless dwellings built in irregular rows—all these are typical of the crowded and haphazard industrial development of the 19th century'.

Exercises

1. Calculate the vertical exaggeration of the section included in the text. Draw a similar cross section from Sart Tilman to Jupille (east of Liège) to show the Ourthe valley and the edge of the Pays de Herve. Label the features crossed by your section line.

2. Using the population totals given on the map extract, construct a map to show the distribution of population in the area by means of proportionate circles. Comment on the inadequacies of such a method as a means of showing population distribution in this particular area. Suggest a classification of the various types of built-up area shown on the map.

3. The following terms appear in the text. Attempt a precise definition of their meaning.
(a) Fault line scarp
(b) Loess
(c) Superimposed drainage
(d) Hercynian orogeny
(e) Braided channel
(f) Geographical inertia.

4. Many of the most important cities in Europe lie at the foot of the Hercynian Foreland. Why should this be so?

5. With the aid of a sketch map, describe and explain the pattern of rail communications in the area covered by the map.

6. Attempt an explanation of the following figures:

Coal output per man/shift 1964 (metric tons)

West Germany	Ruhr	2·680	*Belgium*	Campine	1·980
	Saar	2·616		Sambre/Meuse	1·603
	Lower Saxony	2·115			
	Aachen	1·989	*France*	Nord/Pas de Calais	1·709
				Lorraine	3·113
Netherlands	Limburg	2·140		Centre-Midi	2·016

(Source: 14th General Report of the European Coal and Steel Community, Luxembourg, 1965)

7. Compare and contrast the Borinage, Liège and Campine coalfields of Belgium. Reference should be made to *A Regional Geography of Western Europe* by F. J. Monkhouse, or for more detailed information see *The Belgian Kempenland* by F. J. Monkhouse (Liverpool University Press 1949) and 'Recent developments in the Belgian Borinage: an area of declining coal production in the European Coal and Steel Community' by R. C. Riley *(Geography* no. 228, **50,** Part 3, July 1965).

8. What is the European Coal and Steel Community? Describe the foundation, aims and progress of this organisation.

9. On a base map, showing the main rivers and land over 100 metres, attempt to plot the distribution of industry and mining in the Liège district. Comment on the factors which determine this distribution pattern.

Further reading

Belgium, Naval Intelligence Geographical Handbook Series, 1944, chapter 12.
DICKINSON, R. E. *The West European City: A Geographical Interpretation,* 2nd edn, Routledge and Kegan Paul, 1961.
ELKINS, T. H. 'Liège and the problems of southern Belgium', *Geography,* no. 192, **41,** part 2, April 1956.
MONKHOUSE, F. J. *The Countries of North West Europe,* Longmans, 1965, chapter 9.
MONKHOUSE, F. J. *A Regional Geography of Western Europe,* Longmans, 1965, chapters 8 and 18.
PATERSON, J. H. 'The population of the Ardennes. Present trends and future prospects', *Geography* no. 228, **50,** part 3, July 1965.

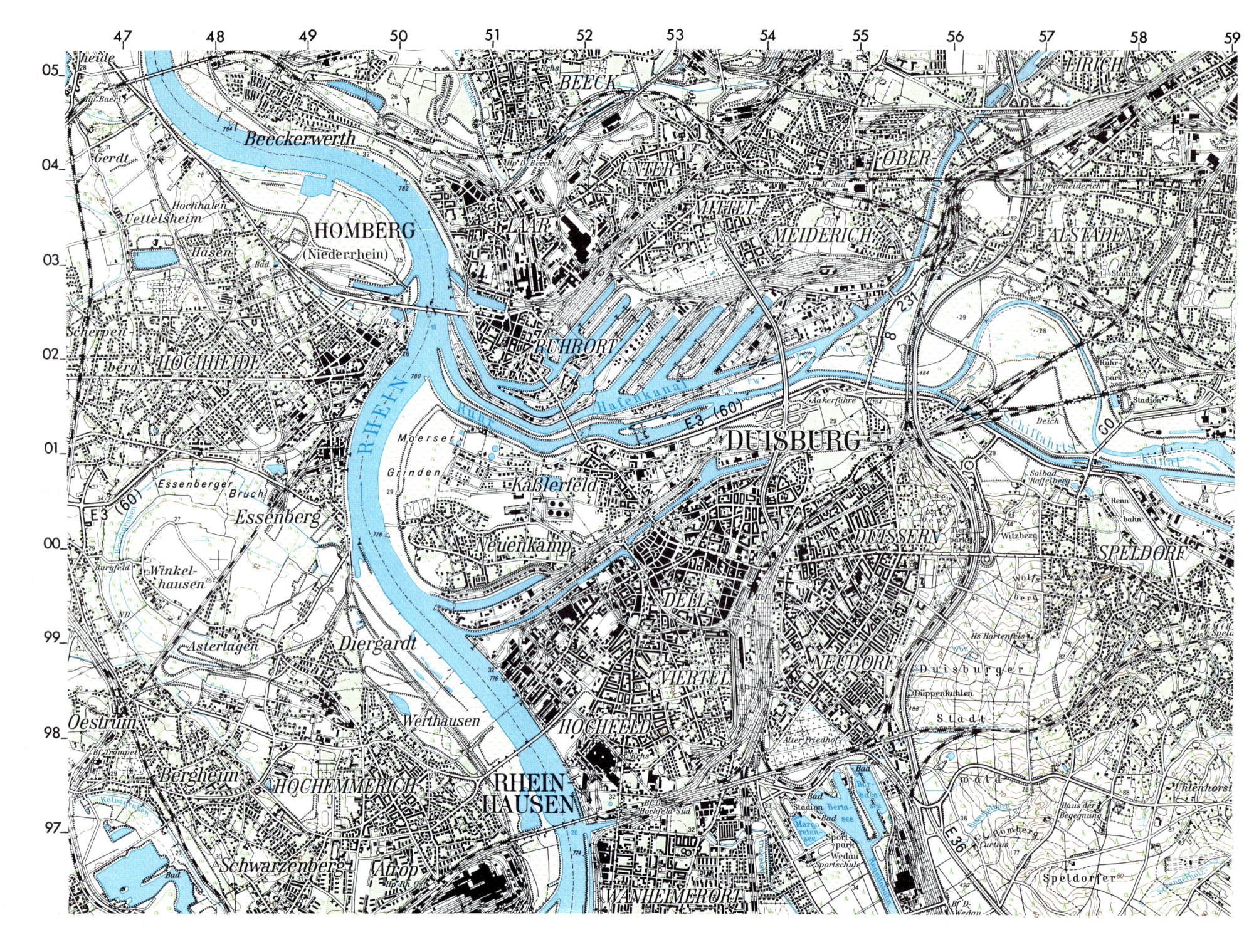

Study 7
DUISBURG-RUHRORT
NORDRHEIN-WESTFALEN
WEST GERMANY

A Section of the Ruhr Conurbation.

Extract from Map Sheet L.4506 Duisburg. West German 1:50,000 Series.

Published 1952.
Revised 1966
Vertical interval of contours 10 metres.
(Form lines at 5 metre and 2.5 metre intervals on gentle slopes)

By permission of Landesvermessungsamt, Nordrhein-Westfalen of 27.11.67 Control No. 2616 reproduced by Longmans, Green & Co. London, W.1.

Photograph 8. The docks at Duisburg-Ruhrort.

German Tourist Information Bureau, London.

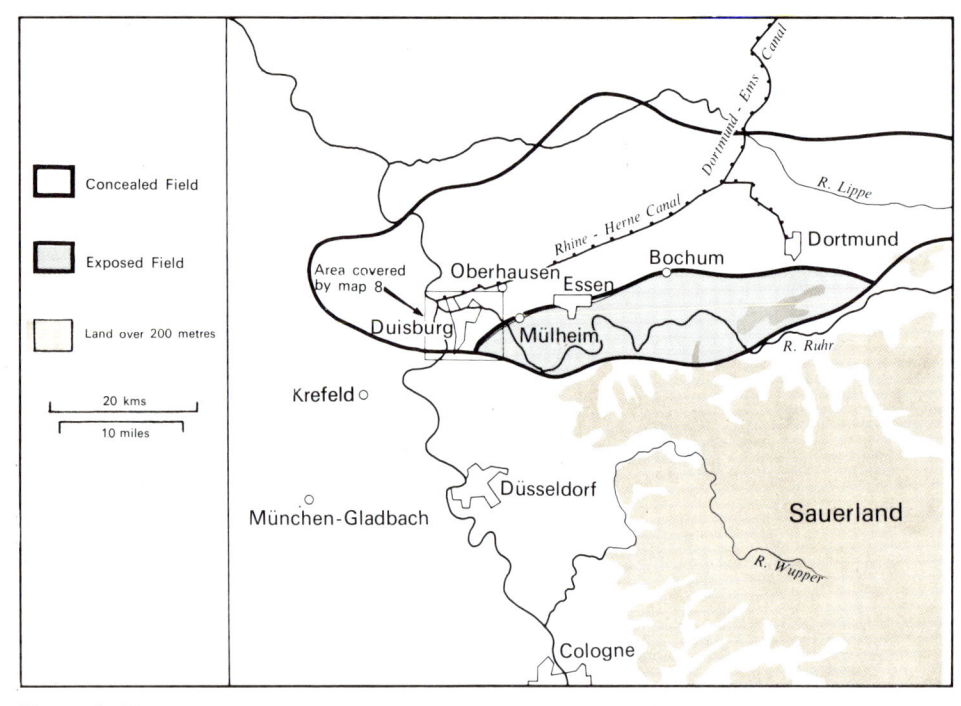

Figure 9. The Ruhr.

The following five studies are based on the West German 1:50,000 series. The style of these maps shows slight variations, according to the Land (province) in which they are published. Relief is expressed by contours or form lines which may have an interval of as little as 2·5 metres on gentle slopes but 10 metres on steeper slopes. Oblique hill shading is employed on the Reutlingen and Kaub sheets.

The landscape shown in map 8 is part of the Rhine valley where it is joined by the River Ruhr from the east. The Rhine at this point is about 25 metres above sea level. Areas of higher land at about 30 metres occur both west of the river, at Hochheide (4702), Oestrum (4798) and Schwarzenberg (4896), and east of the Rhine at Hochfeld and Dellviertal (5298). Further to the east there is an abrupt rise to summit heights of about 75 to 80 metres on the Kaiserberg, Wolfsberg and Homberg (5500, 5699, 5697). These summits are at similar levels, but the sides of the hill masses are steep and deeply dissected by small streams. Although the actual map evidence is not abundant, the relief suggests a flood plain with terraces above it which relate to various phases of the Rhine's history (see Study 9). The plain on either side of the Rhine shows considerable evidence of liability to flooding and of changes of channel. West of the Rhine between Essenberg (4800) and Hochemmerich (4897) lies a loop of land followed by the Bruchgraben. This is seamed with drainage channels and is covered with bushes and reeds. The shape of the loop suggests an abandoned meander. Along both sides of the Rhine and Ruhr the frequency of banks or dykes indicates the need to protect settlements from flooding. Quite wide stretches of land are shown to be covered only with reeds. This, in an area of dense settlement and high land values, suggests that flooding is a very real possibility.

Land use

Both map and photographs show a landscape dominated by industry and commerce. Photograph 8 is of the docks at Duisburg-Ruhrort, while photograph 9 shows the Rhine at Duisburg with a multitude of factories and chimneys clustering along the river's right bank.

Duisburg lies at the eastern end of the Ruhr, undoubtedly the most industrialised region of Germany and possibly of Europe. To the south of

Photograph 9. The Rhine front at Duisburg.
German Tourist Information Bureau, London.

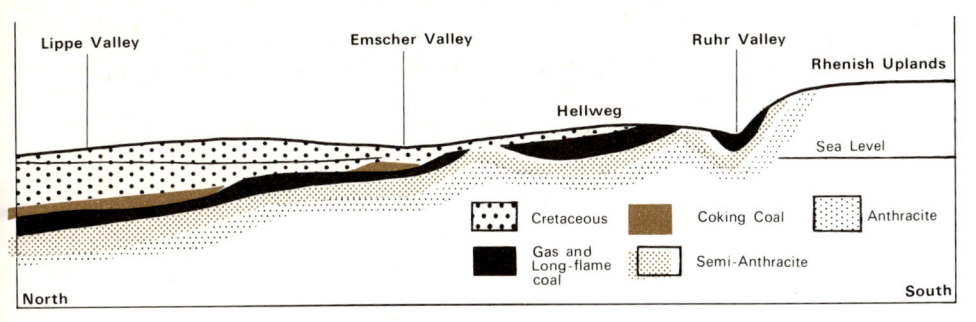

Figure 10. Generalised section across the Ruhr coalfield *(after T. H. Elkins.)*

the Ruhr lie the Hercynian mountains of Germany (Sauerland, Westerwald); to the north are the infertile gravels, sands and marshes of the North German Plain (see Study 11). Between the two lies the loess belt, with its light and porous soils which have proved attractive to farmers over many centuries. In the Middle Ages this belt constituted an important routeway between France and Belgium to the west and Saxony and Silesia to the east. To the south of Duisburg the Rhine provided the most important routeway through the Hercynian uplands. Thus the area has long been important as a cross-roads. Cologne first arose under the Romans, whilst Duisburg, Essen and Dortmund, lying on this east to west route (the Hellweg), had some significance as Hanse cities in the 14th and 15th centuries.

The tradition of manufacturing can likewise be traced back to medieval times. The Siegerland hills to the south, with their supplies of iron ore, their woods to provide charcoal and their water power from fast flowing streams, have a long history of metal working. Indeed, in 1800 this hill region was one of the most important iron working centres in Europe. The advent of the blast-furnace, using coke, heralded the development of the Ruhr region itself as a major metal working area.

The Ruhr coalfield consists of a series of basins with a north-east strike. To the south, on the flanks of the hill country, the coal measures are exposed, but north of a line from Duisburg to Bochum they are overlain by Cretaceous strata (to a depth of 1,400 metres near Münster). There are some 57 workable seams within the field having a total thickness of 200 feet. Two-thirds of the production is best coking coal, one-fifth is gas coal, and less than one-twentieth is poor quality coal. Though seams are faulted and sometimes difficult to work, nevertheless the wide variety of coal, the thickness of seams and the enormous reserves have given the region an excellent base for manufacturing industry. A few mines are shown in operation near Duisburg, including the Diergardt (489983), and Altstaden (580018 and 571041) mines which produce anthracite. However, most coal is now produced in mines much further to the north. Indeed evidence for the decline in mining is shown on the map near Hochheide, where two disused mines are depicted (488015 and 477011).

The first blast furnace was built in the Ruhr at Mülheim (2 km east of the map extract) in 1849. Although home supplies of ore were at first sufficient (principally from the Lahn, Dill and Siegerland districts south of the Ruhr), foreign supplies became more important after 1860. With the invention of the Gilchrist-Thomas basic process in 1879 for using phosphoric ores, the Ruhr was able to make use of the Minette ores of Lorraine, which was at that time part of Germany. However, by 1913 Swedish ores had become of greater importance: transport from Lorraine was difficult and the Minette ores were of low grade. Smelting in Lorraine using Ruhr coke became more profitable than moving Lorraine ore for smelting to the Ruhr. In 1902 the Narvik railway was constructed, reducing the cost of Lapland ore. Thus a connection was established between Sweden and the Ruhr which has persisted to the present day (see Study 3).

Imports of iron ore into Western Germany 1965 (1,000 metric tons)

Country of origin		Country of origin		Total imports 1965
Sweden	9,952	Venezuela	1,944	
France	5,927	Peru	1,601	35,471
Liberia	5,776	Mauretania	1,240	
Brazil	3,357			

(1966 *Statistical Handbook on Iron and Steel,* Statistical Office, European Communities.)

The above figures stress the reliance that West Germany places upon imported supplies of ore. In the same year her own domestic production amounted to 10,847 thousand metric tons. This situation has tended to attract the industries towards the routes along which the ore travels. The largest plants in the Ruhr region are to be found in Duisburg-Hamborn-Ruhrort-Meiderich, Mülheim, Oberhausen and Essen. All except Essen are served by the Rhine and the canals which lead from it. Greater Duisburg is on the Rhine itself; Mülheim is linked to the Rhine by the ship canal marked on the eastern side of the map extract; Oberhausen lies adjacent to the Rhein-Herne canal which leaves the map in the north-east. The eastern area is typified by Dortmund; this is connected to the sea at Emden by the Dortmund-Ems canal, but is rather less important than the western region based on the Rhine. The map shows several iron and steel producing works. Their names and distribution can be ascertained by reference to fig. 11.

Significantly, all of them lie close to navigable waterways and indeed they sometimes possess their own private docks. In comparison with much British plant, they are large and usually of an integrated type, i.e. blast-furnaces, steel furnaces and finishing plant lie adjacent to each other within the same works area. In the case of the Phoenix works in Ruhrort, the coal and coke producing plant is on the same site, but for other works coke has to come from further afield.

The coke works also provide the basis for an important chemical industry. In Meiderich, for example, coal tar distillation plant produces a wide range of products including pitch, oil, creosote, sulphate of ammonia, dyestuffs and raw materials for explosives and pharmaceutical products. The locations of many chemical works are shown on fig. 11 and the importance of a location near to waterways or railways for the transport of bulky goods is again apparent. The petrochemical industry has shown spectacular growth in recent years, and it is significant that since 1961 a large area of land has been taken over for this purpose south of the mouth of the Ruhr river.

In addition to the basic manufacture of coke, iron, steel and chemicals, there is a wide range of other industries in this region, many of which draw their raw materials from the iron and steel industries. Particularly important are the metal, construction and engineering industries. A comparison between fig. 11 and the map extract will reveal at least some of the reasons behind their locations.

Settlement and communications

Settlement in the area of the map extract appears to be almost continuous except for the difficult areas of the river flood plains and the steep wooded hills of the south-east. Greater Duisburg includes Ruhrort, Meiderich and Hamborn (to the north of Ruhrort) and had a population of 496,000 in 1964. Duisburg itself originated as a fortress at a crossing point of the Rhine about A.D. 700. In medieval times it grew to considerable importance as a trading town on the important east-west route known as the Hellweg. The old town can be recognised at 5300 on the south side of the Innenhafen. In those days the Rhine pursued a more easterly course and the town benefited from its proximity. The extension of Duisburg was rapid in the 19th century when industrialisation became important, but its growth was limited to the east by the hills of the Kaiserberg. Today there is a marked zoning of function which is easily seen on the map. Along the banks of the Rhine, by the harbours, and by the side of the railways leading to the Rhine lies an area mainly given over to industry. Photograph 9 shows the vast extent of the waterside industry by the Rhine. To the east of the main railway in Duissern and Neudorf and to the south of the old city lie the main residential areas. Duisburg, however, does not seem to be without its amenities. In contrast to some of the older industrial cities of Britain, a large amount of open space still persists. In practically all the residential districts the symbol for a garden is widely shown, while in the south a large Sports Park is to be found with a stadium, swimming and boating and other facilities.

Ruhrort is of later growth. Its beginnings lay in the 14th century when a castle on an island in the Rhine exacted tolls on river traffic. A nearby fishing village became associated with the castle, and eventually walls were built.

Figure 11. Duisburg: Industrial location map.   (Drawn at half the scale of Map 8.)

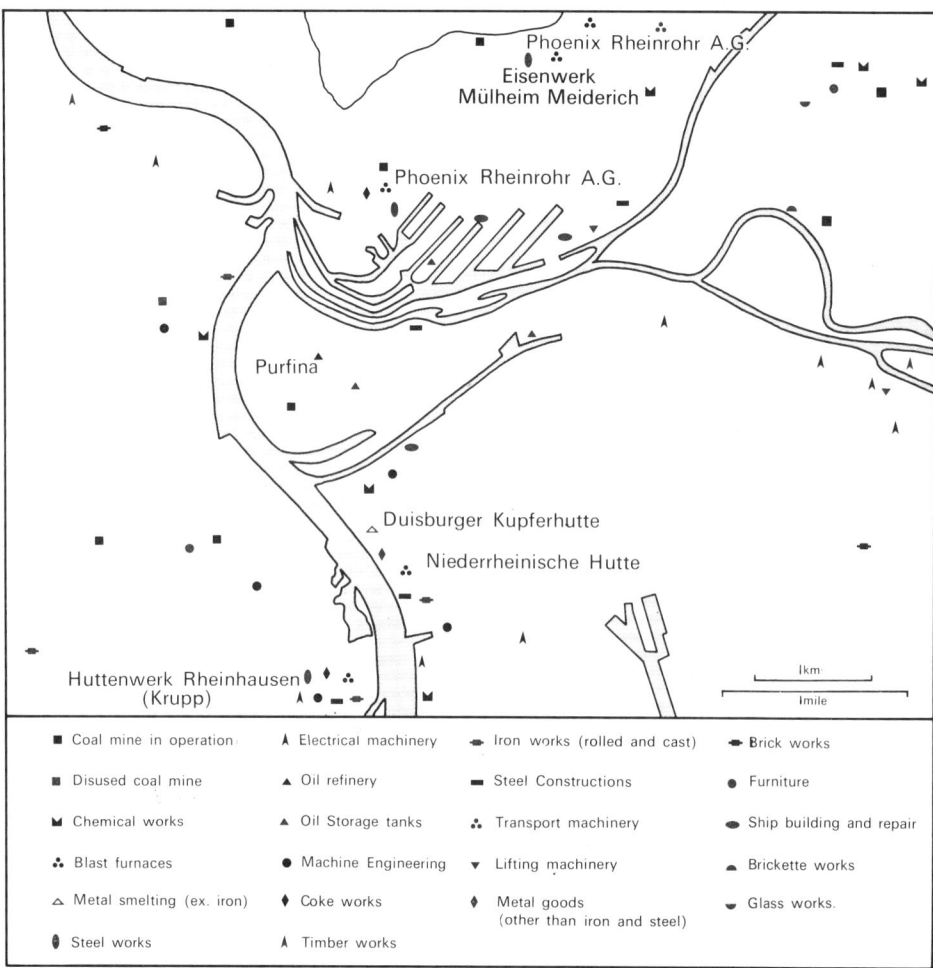

This formed the Altstadt (510018). To the north the Neustadt was laid out in the latter part of the 19th century. This followed the improvement of navigation on the River Ruhr which allowed coal traffic to reach the Rhine from mines in the south.

The growth of Duisburg and Ruhrort has been largely a result of improvements in communications, many of which date from the 19th century. The complex of harbours, railway lines, canals and roads has enabled the area to become a major transport centre for much of the industrialised Ruhr region. The construction of docks was obviously facilitated by the soft stretches of alluvium found in the flood plains. Though most of these were built in the 19th century, the three harbours north of the Hafenkanal were completed only in 1908. The linkage of the port to its hinterland in the Ruhr was effected by the construction of the Rhein-Herne canal in 1914 and of a canalised channel to Mülheim. The growth of traffic through the ports of Duisburg-Ruhrort was particularly marked from 1880 onwards.

Total Goods Traffic (1000 metric tons)

1875	1895	1905	1927	1937
2,935	7,416	19,462	33,567	34,297

(These figures refer to the entire Duisburg harbours including Schwelgern in the north and Huckingen in the south. The figures in Ex. 5 refer solely to the Duisburg-Ruhrort harbours on the extract).

During the 1939–45 war many of the harbour installations were badly damaged but after a long period of recovery the figure reached 30 million tons in 1957, and in 1965 stood at 32 million tons.

Photograph 8 shows the vast spread of the docks at the mouth of the River Ruhr. At the top right-hand corner the lock entrances can be seen to both the canalised River Ruhr and the Rhein-Herne canal. The docks are mainly concerned with bulky products of generally low value. Ruhrort dominates the coal export trade and imports large quantities of iron ore. There is also evidence on the photograph of a third important cargo, namely oil.

The docks in Duisburg, significantly, have no connection with the Ruhr and the Rhein-Herne canals. Timber, cotton, wool and grain are important cargoes. Their destination may be factories in Duisburg or distribution to the rest of Germany by rail.

Communication by railway is of great significance in the Duisburg area. A close network of lines links the dock, warehouse and factory area with cities in the Ruhr and beyond. The pattern follows the ancient east-west lines of communication and the north-south Rhine route. In T. H. Elkins's words: 'At the mouth of the Ruhr river, the Hercynian foreland and the Rhine routeways intersect: there could not possibly be a more favourable situation for the development of a coalfield and the growth of an industrial region than at this crossroads of Europe'.

Exercises

1. Examine the changing significance of factors in the location of the iron and steel industries of West Germany and Britain.
2. Calculate the length of docking space in Duisburg-Ruhrort on the map extract, and compare with that of Marseilles (map 16). Comment on your result, relating it to the types of traffic entering and leaving the ports.
3. Construct a flow diagram for iron ore movement to West Germany. Comment on sources and scale of movement.
4. 'In the Ruhr region the road system is antiquated, tortuous and frequently congested by tram lines, this being neither convenient nor important for anything but local traffic' (A. Mutton). Comment on this quotation in relation to the map extract.

5. *Total goods traffic (1,000 metric tons)*

	1936	1964
Total	17,366	16,188
Coal	12,226	3,305
Ores	1,250	4,602
Iron	363	1,459
Scrap	367	846
Grain	295	259
Provisions	187	85
Wood	223	28
Gravel/Sand	1,529	670
Mineral Oil	209	3,157
Refined Minerals	259	631
Fertiliser	194	467
Other goods	263	529
Local traffic	—	149

Source: Niederrheinische Industrie und Handelskammer. Duisburg Wesel.

The above figures show imports and exports for the Duisburg-Ruhrort harbours. Construct a suitable diagram to express these figures and comment upon the changes in trade patterns that they reveal.

6. Give an account of the industrial geography of the Ruhr. (W.J.E.C.)
7. Examine the influence of water transport on the industrial development of the Ruhr. (J.M.B.)

Further reading

DICKINSON, R. E. *Germany: A General and Regional Geography*, Methuen, 1953, chapter 18.
ELKINS, T. H. *Germany*, Chatto & Windus, 1968, chapter 15.
Germany, vols III and IV, Naval Intelligence Geographical Handbooks Series, 1944–5.
HALL, P. *The World Cities*, World University Library, Weidenfeld and Nicolson, 1966, chapter 5.
HARRIS, C. D. 'The Ruhr coal mining district', *Geographical Review* **36**, 1946.
POUNDS, N. J. G. *The Geography of Iron and Steel*, Hutchinson's University Library, 1968.
POUNDS, N. J. G. *The Ruhr: A Study in Historical and Economic Geography*, Faber, 1952.
POUNDS, N. J. G. and PARKER, W. N. *Coal and Steel in Western Europe*, Faber, 1957.

Study 8
REUTLINGEN BADEN-WÜRTTEMBURG WEST GERMANY
A Part of the South German Scarplands

Relief

The area shown in map 9 is part of the South German Scarplands. Its location may be seen in fig. 12.

Analysis of the map reveals a landscape of considerable variation in relief. From north-east to south-west runs a well marked scarp slope. This divides the high Alb country of over 650 metres from the lower region to the north-west. The Alb country (part of the Swäbischealb) is gently rolling and diversified by a series of knolls and depressions. Thus, south-east of Albgut Lindenhof lies a large depression enclosed by the 697·5 metre contour containing fourteen separate small pits or hollows. Elsewhere many knolls are a feature of the landscape. These are often rounded in plan and reach a height of 50 metres above the surrounding plateau. The most striking features of the scarp slope are its steepness and marked indentation. Long steep-sided valleys penetrate into the plateau and are separated by flat-topped spurs. In the south the valley of the River Echaz penetrates many miles into the Alb to provide a routeway to the plateau. In some cases erosion has proceeded still further, and outliers are left away from the main scarp. Two excellent examples are Achalm and Rangenbergle. These may be readily identified on photograph 11. In the same picture the level plateau surface and the steep scarp slope are apparent. In photograph 10 the flat-topped spurs of Urselberg and Alsberg stand out at the foot of the picture while the isolated peak of Achalm is just visible to the right. The indentation of the scarp is largely a result of spring sapping and river erosion. The large number of springs marked along the scarp slope, and particularly at the heads of the valleys, gives some indication of the height of outcrops of impervious strata.

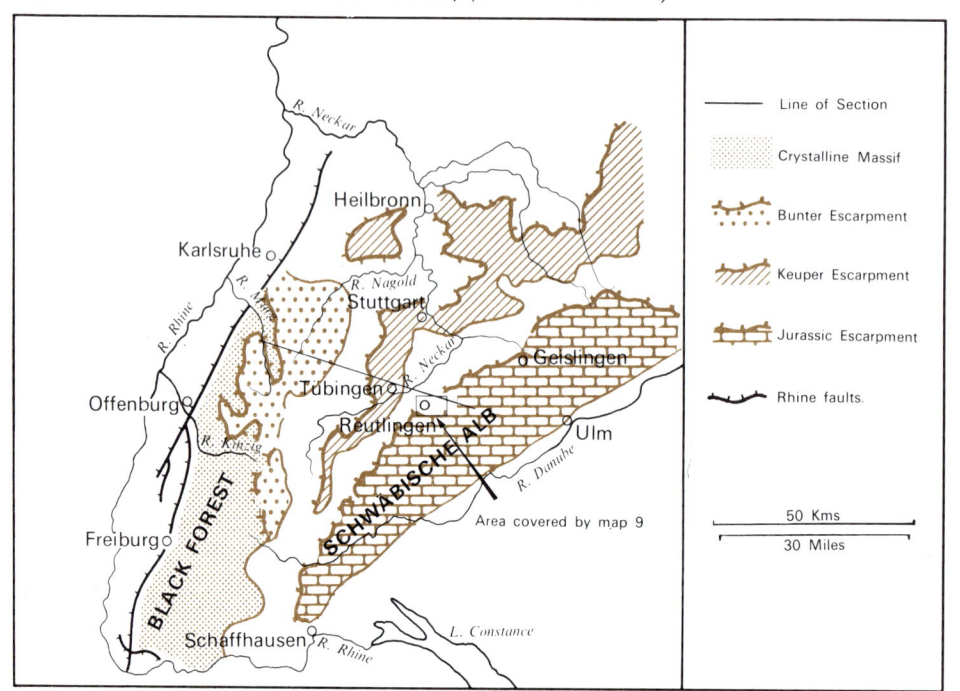

The landscape north-east of the scarp slope is lower. The Echaz pursues a meandering course towards the north-west, falling from approximately 500 metres at Unterhausen to 320 metres at Stockach, an average gradient of 1 in 81. A series of small streams drains into the Echaz, usually from north-east or south-west. These divide the landscape into a series of parallel, arcuate ridges. The most striking of these is that which runs from Spitalwald to Georgenberg, is then cut by the Echaz valley but continues on the north-east side to Scheibenberg and Endschliff. The height of this ridge is over 500 metres, and the steep, dissected north-west side with the more gentle south-east slope gives it the character of an escarpment.

The obvious physical contrasts within this map extract have their origin in the rocks of which the landscape is made. The absence of surface drainage, the steep scarp slope and the height of the plateau in the east and south indicate a rock of pervious and resistant quality. In contrast a less permeable and less resistant material is indicated in the lower land to the north-west. The South German scarplands are formed of Mesozoic or Secondary rocks, laid down in a great basin east of the Black Forest. They were affected by earth movements during the Alpine mountain-building period, strongly in the south-west but more gently towards the north-east. Thus near the southern end of the Black Forest the strata are steeply dipping with narrow outcrops, while further to the north-east the dip is far less and outcrops are broader. The section in fig. 13 shows the various rock types across the scarplands from W.N.W. to E.S.E. The upper Oolitic or Jurassic strata which compose the high Alb plateau (White Jura) include two layers of limestone with intervening marly beds. These limestones are the scarp formers and responsible for the imposing escarpment in the east and south of the extract. The protection afforded by one of these strata is also responsible for the preservation of outliers such as Achalm, though erosion along a fault line has resulted in the severance of this particular outlier. Below the Malm beds of the White Jura outcrop the Dogger beds which form the Brown Jura. These correspond in age to our Lower Oolites, but unlike the British Lower Oolites they are predominantly argillaceous. However, the occurrence of a resistant ironstone bed *(Eisensandstein)*, and above it a resistant

Figure 12. The structure of S.W. Germany *(after T. H. Elkins.)*

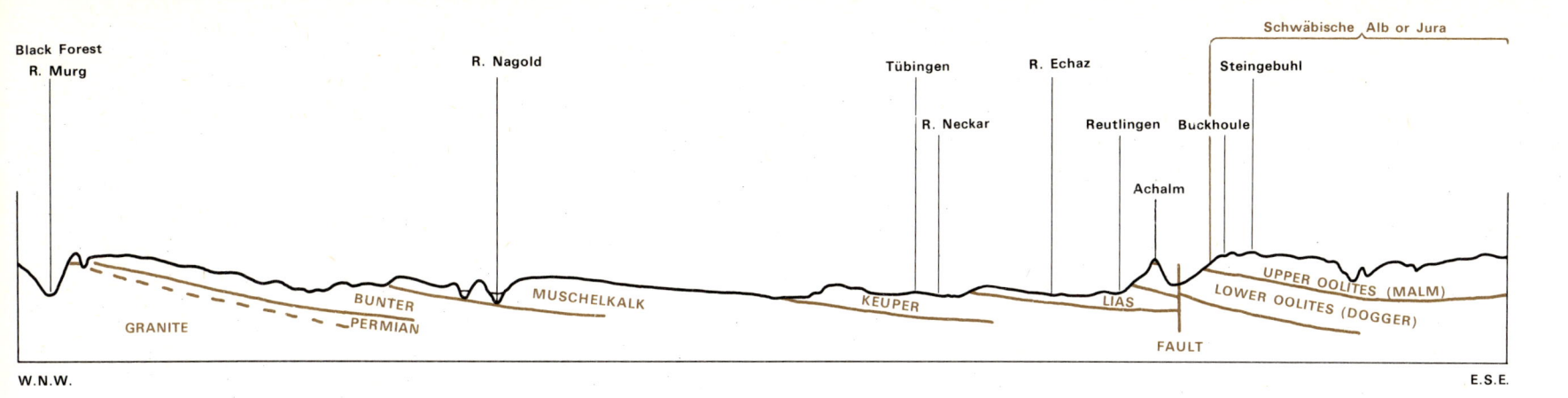

Figure 13. Section from W.N.W. to E.S.E. across the south German Scarplands (after T. H. Elkins.)

limestone, gives rise to the steep lower slopes of the main scarp and the scarp between Spitalwald and Endschliff including the lower slopes of Achalm. The Liassic beds which form the lower lands around Reutlingen consist mainly of dark clays and shales. These form the Black Jura and are less resistant than the Oolite series, though a few limestone bands occasionally produce small escarpments.

Land use

Soils in this region are closely related to geology. The high Alb plateau has rendzina soils developed on the limestone. Though some arable cultivation is practised, most of the land not under woodland is devoted to pasture. The symbol for rough pasture is frequently to be seen (note Eninger Weide, east of Eningen). Most of the knolls and the steeper slopes of the plateau are under woodland. It is interesting to note that there is a mixture of deciduous and coniferous trees. Originally most of the high plateau was under beech; the conifers are an introduction by man and reflect the marginal quality of much of this land for agriculture. Both map and photographs indicate that soils in the valleys are frequently of good quality. The large open fields with their distinctive pattern of strips and absence of hedges stand out particularly well in photograph 10. These areas coincide with beds of the Brown Jura, though the addition of calcareous material by downwash has no doubt improved them. Agriculture in these lower areas is very mixed. Both arable and pastoral areas are to be seen, while the regular spacing of many of the trees suggests that fruit production is important. However, the number of people engaged in agriculture has declined in recent years. This is a trend observable in practically every western European country, and is the result of increasing industrialisation together with the development of labour saving farming methods. The proportion of agricultural workers compared with the total working population in Landkreis Reutlingen fell from 21·3 per cent in 1939 to 9·1 per cent in 1960 and 6·7 per cent in 1964. Most farms in the area are family concerns and predominantly rather small, as the following figures indicate.

Farms grouped by size in Landkreis Reutlingen (1960)

Hectares		Hectares	
0·5– 2	47·5%	10–20	3·8%
2 – 5	31·4%	20–50	0·5%
5 – 7·5	12·4%	50–100	0·15%
7·5–10	4·2%	Over 100	0·05%

Source: Industrie—und Handelskammer. Reutlingen.

Settlement

Settlement in this region dates from very early times. The suffix *-ingen* indicates that these were settlements of early Allemanic tribes. Daughter settlements were established at a later stage and the suffixes *-hausen* or *-dorf* are often an indication of these villages.

Settlement on the Alb plateau tends to be nucleated, though a few isolated buildings are shown. Ohnastetten, with between 40 and 50 houses, is built on a gentle slope at about 758 metres. There is no evidence of a water supply, but no doubt the water table is at such a depth that the sinking of wells is possible. Several of the isolated buildings are inns (*Wirtshaus*, abb. *Whs.*) and their activity stems from the obvious scenic attractions of the scarpland. The foot of the main scarp provides an excellent site for settlement. Glems is situated in a small, sheltered valley at a height of between 420 and 440 metres with the advantage of a plentiful water supply. Eningen is in a similar situation, though the valley is wider and gently sloping land for building more abundant. The rectilinear road pattern south-west of Eningen

49

REUTLINGEN
BADEN-
WÜRTTEMBURG
WEST GERMANY

Extract from Map Sheet L.7520. Reutlingen. West German 1:50,000 Series.

Published 1958. Revised 1964. Vertical interval of contours 10 metres. (Form lines at 5 metre and 2.5 metre intervals on gentle slopes.)

Extract from Topographical map 1:50,000 sheet L7520 by permission of Landesvermessungsamt. Baden—Württemberg.

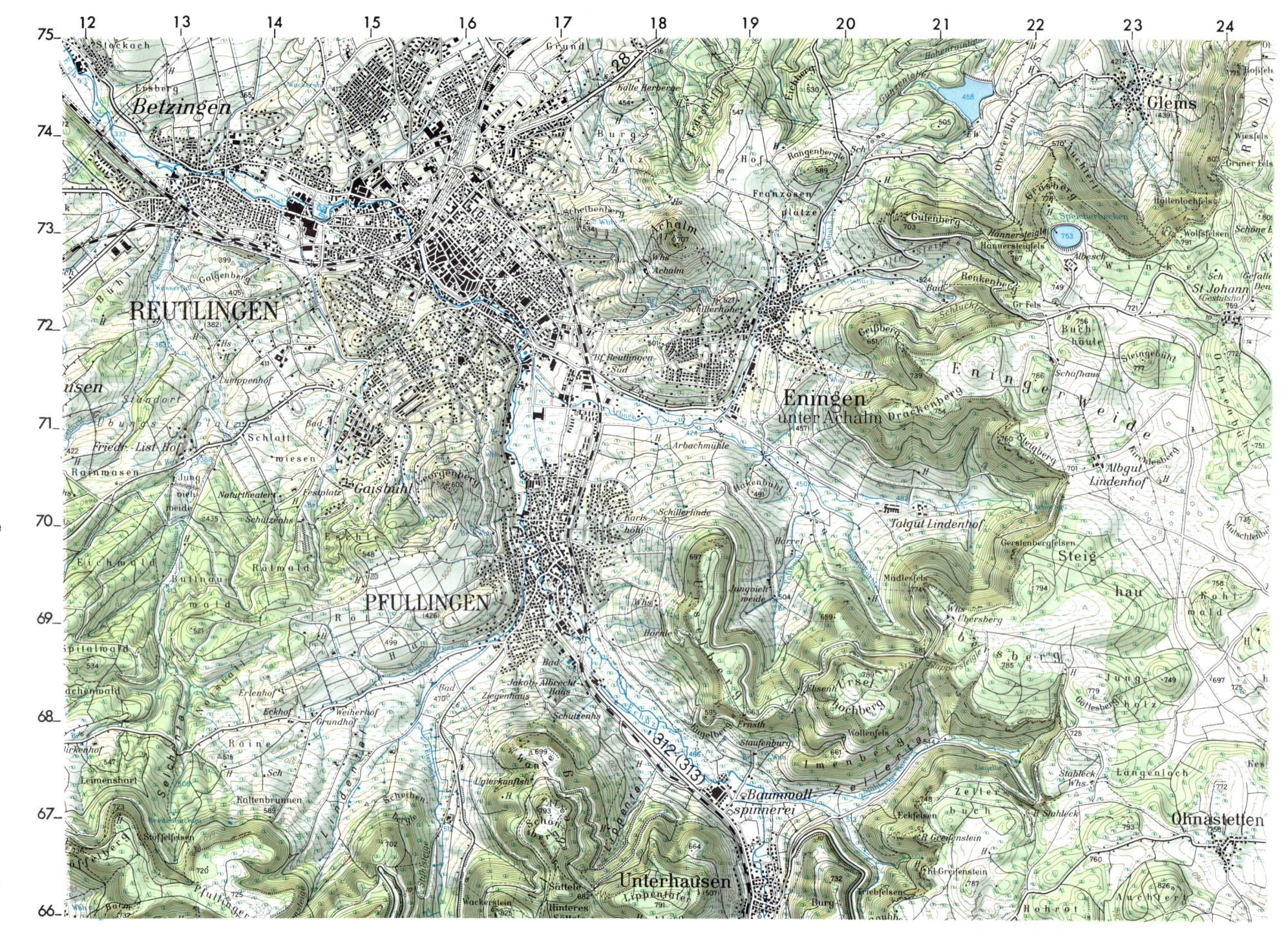

Map 9

Photograph 10. Reutlingen and Pfullingen.

Albrecht Brugger, Stuttgart.

seems to indicate a modern development. Pfullingen and Unterhausen are both sited on gently sloping land by the River Echaz. The core of Pfullingen can be identified on the map and on photograph 10 as a zone of twisting and narrow streets. Outside the town, modern residential developments have taken advantage of the gentle slopes of the hills to the east and south-west. Photograph 11 shows the character of this housing. Usually single storey, but occasionally double, their steeply pitched roofs are characteristic of much building in Swabia and indeed in south Germany. Unterhausen is situated further up the Echaz valley where the sides are steeper (1 in 4) and the valley floor narrower (c. ⅓ km) though still flat. It tends to assume, therefore, a more elongated shape and far less modern building has taken place.

The region of the map extract, with a belt of land stretching north to the Neckar valley, is dominated by the town of Reutlingen. This is an ancient settlement sited on the north-east side of a bend in the River Echaz. The core of the town (once walled and moated) is shown on the map in black shading and shows clearly on photograph 10 as a crowded zone of narrow streets. Outside this central area settlement follows a different pattern. To the north-east is a region of rectilinear streets including houses, factories, woodland and gardens. Further to the north-east, on the slopes of Scheibenberg, the density of housing is still lower. A similar pattern is seen in other directions, though in Gaisbühl some apartment blocks have been constructed.

The reasons for the growth of Reutlingen and Pfullingen can be partially inferred from the map and photograph 11. Throughout the Echaz valley, usually adjacent to the river, is a number of factories. These can be identified on the map by black shading and by the symbol for a factory chimney. The nature of these factories is shown only in one place, just north of Unterhausen, where *'Baumwoll spinnerei'* indicates a textile factory. Originally the interest lay in wool, but in the nineteenth century cotton became the main concern and factories were built to use the water power provided by the fast flowing scarp-foot streams. Today coal and electricity are the main sources of power. The variety of goods produced is very wide. It includes knitwear and woven articles, underclothing, towelling, sports clothing, suitings and dress materials as well as woven silk goods and sewing cottons. The success of the textile industry has encouraged the growth of various linked industries. Thus Reutlingen is an important centre for textile machinery, including knitting machines. A third group of industries is concerned with metal and engineering and includes paper machinery, machine tools, electrical machinery, cameras and electronic measuring devices. Finally, a group of miscellaneous industries includes veneers, plastics, leather and leather goods, printing and publishing.

A second important factor in the growth of Reutlingen and Pfullingen lies in the ease of communications and hence the availability of raw materials, fuels and markets. The railway which leaves Reutlingen to the north-east goes to Stuttgart, while to the north-west the line continues to Tübingen. The route across the Alb is of less importance (note the single track status) but provides a link with Ulm and the Danube valley. Roads follow a similar pattern. The N.28 joins Ulm, Reutlingen, Tübingen and the Rhine valley, with important links to Stuttgart and the autobahn network, while the N.312 crosses the Alb plateau to the Danube valley. Other roads are of local significance and show a close relationship to relief in their routes.

Reutlingen and Pfullingen are today very prosperous towns. An indication of their rate of growth is given by the following population figures:

	1946	**1950**	**1961**	**1966**
Reutlingen	38,468	45,753	67,407	73,437
Pfullingen	9,453	11,353	13,598	14,971

The large increase since 1950 is mostly due to the rapid growth of the textile industry and its associated industries, and to the ready markets available for their high quality goods.

Exercises

1. Draw a detailed sketch map of the town of Reutlingen and its suburb Betzingen. Shade in areas devoted to different uses, i.e. central business district, old residential, new residential, factories. Explain the factors which have guided the expansion of the town.
2. Describe the various types of land use which can be identified from the two photographs. How far does the map add to the information so obtained?
3. Draw a profile of the landscape along a straight line from Stockach in the north-west corner of the map, through Achalm, to the eastern margin of the map. Below the appropriate part of your profile write brief (single word if possible) descriptions of (a) land form; (b) drainage; (c) land use; (d) settlement; (e) communications.
    Comment on the relationships revealed.
4. Discuss the relationship between roads and relief in the area of the map.
5. Refer to a 1:63360 map of the Cotswolds (Sheet 144). Discuss the similarities and differences in landforms between the Alb scarp and the Cotswold scarp.
6. Plot the heights of springs on the Alb scarp and along the valleys which dissect it. What conclusions can you draw from your information?
7. By identifying points on photograph 10 and comparing their distances apart, calculate the scale of the photograph (a) in the centre; (b) along one of the edges. What is the maximum percentage scale error on this aerial photograph?

Further reading

DICKINSON, R. E. Germany. *A Regional and Economic Geography*, Methuen 1963, chapter 22.
ELKINS, T. H. *Germany*, Chatto & Windus, 1968, chapter 11.
ELKINS, T. H. and YATES, E. M. 'The South German scarplands in the vicinity of Tübingen', **18** pt. 4, *Geography* 221, November 1963.

Photograph 11. Pfullingen. Notice the main alb scarp and the Achalm outlier.

Albrecht Brugger, Stuttgart.

Study 9
KAUB
RHINELAND-PFALZ
WEST GERMANY

A Section of the Rhine Gorge.

Extract from Map Sheet L.5912. Kaub. West German 1:50,000 Series.

Published 1960.
Vertical interval of contours 10 metres.
(Form lines at 5 metre and 2.5 metre intervals on gentle slopes.)

By permission of Landesvermessungsamt Rheinland-Pfalz.

Map 10

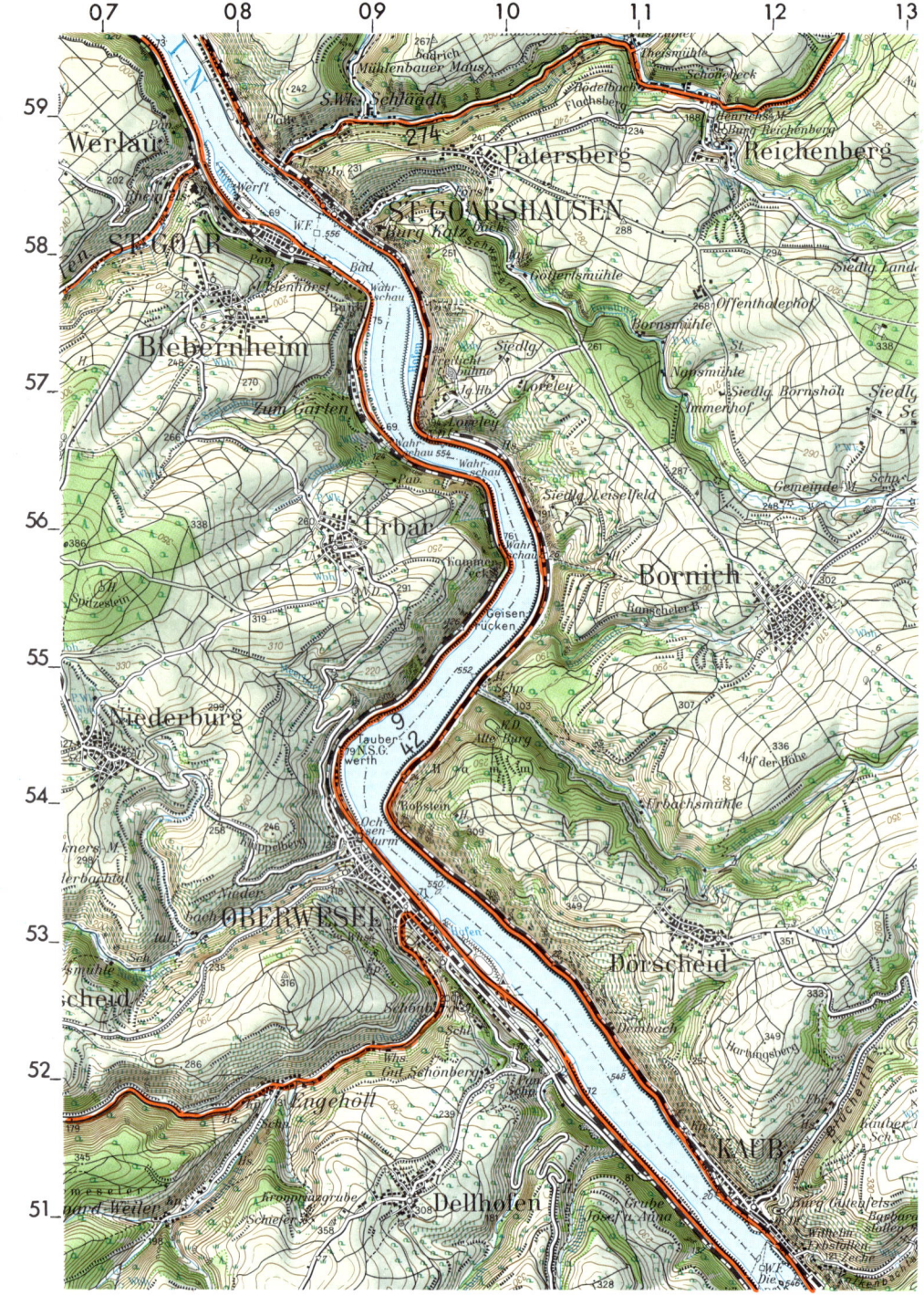

Relief

The map extract shows part of the southern end of the Rhine gorge between Bingen and Koblenz. The hill summits away from the river are rather flat and usually at heights of between 330 and 390 metres. This observation is confirmed by the photograph, where the uniformity of the even skyline is quite remarkable. Several deep and steep-sided valleys are cut into this plateau. These generally follow north-east to south-west courses, but sections at right angles to this direction are occasionally found. The course of the Urbach (1053) illustrates this point. The Rhine flows in a general south-east to north-west direction and occupies a valley which is notable for the steepness of its sides. Slopes of 1 in 1 (45°) may be calculated and confirmed on the photograph. However, the gradient of the river itself is comparatively slight. Spot heights are marked along the road on the west bank and, although one cannot be certain of the height of the road above the river, it is clear that the Rhine falls by no more than 3 metres in the 8 km from just below Kaub to St Goar, a gradient of 1 in 2666. This order of gradient is usually associated with rivers with wide floodplains, yet there is little evidence of floodplain development. Indeed, settlements are narrow and elongated, and there is often little space for the road and railway.

Reference to fig. 14 will show the abnormal character of the Rhine valley. Above Mainz, the river occupies a wide and flat valley. After a short east-north-east to west-south-west section below Mainz, it turns north-west and cuts through the Rhine Highlands in a narrow steep-sided gorge, part of which is represented in the extract. Near Bonn, the river leaves this gorge and enters another section with a wide floodplain.

The Rhine Highlands consist of the Eifel, Westerwald, Taunus and Hunsrück Uplands, and are the product of the Hercynian mountain building period. Far older than the Alps, these uplands have undergone considerable periods of erosion in the 320 million years of their history. The flat plateau tops on the extract represent a peneplain surface formed at an earlier stage of the river's history. It is thought that as this peneplain was uplifted to its present height, the river managed to cut down at a similar rate and so preserve its northward course. Thus the Rhine today flows from a plain, through a gorge, and beyond to a second plain section.

The steep-sided tributary valleys are also a consequence of incision by the Rhine. As the Rhine eroded its valley, so the tributary streams which find their base levels in the main stream also cut into the peneplain. Near the Rhine the processes of vertical corrasion have produced valleys with extremely steep sides, but further upstream the downcutting has not proceeded so far, and valley sides are more gentle. The steep gradients in the

Photograph 12. The Rhine Gorge and the Loreley.

German Tourist Information Bureau, London.

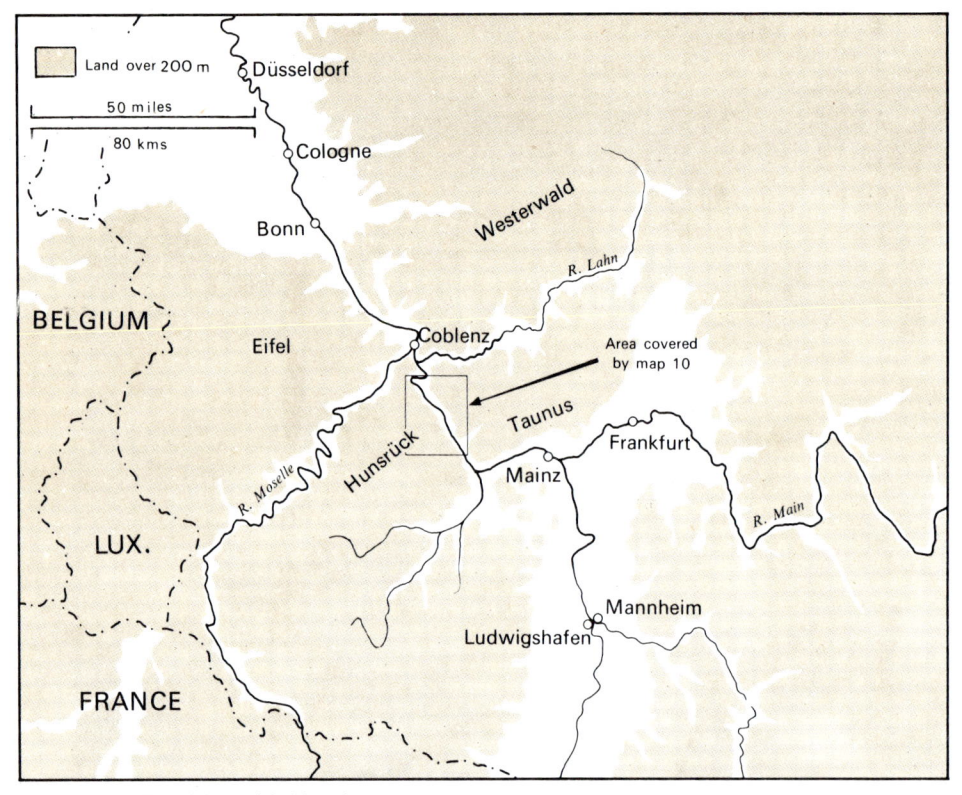

Figure 14. The Rhine highlands.

lower tributary valleys (Schweizertal 1 in 25) seem to have encouraged the establishment of mills although the narrowness of the valley floors precludes much settlement.

Land use

The West German 1:50,000 map series does not give the degree of detail of land use which is to be found on the corresponding Dutch sheets (see Study 5). However, certain broad distinctions can be made between various areas on the map extract. The flat tops of the plateau appear to be divided between farmland and woodland. From the close network of roads it seems clear that the non-wooded land is used for farming. Although the map does not distinguish between arable land and pasture, the photograph (top right) suggests that pasture is more common than plough. Lower, reference to *Germany* by R. E. Dickinson (map, p. 430) shows that on either side of the Rhine there are stretches of the lower part of the plateau which are covered with loess. This is of relatively recent origin, and produces a loamy soil suitable for arable farming.

The other major form of land use in the area is the growing of vines. A study of map and photograph indicates that the gradient and aspect of slopes are of considerable importance in this respect. In practically every case, vines are to be found on south, south-west, or occasionally south-east facing slopes, a particularly fine example being along the north side of the Oberbach valley in its course west of Oberwesel. Frequently these slopes reach gradients of 1 in 1, and the symbol for a bank or wall shows the necessity for terracing to hold the earth in place. Nevertheless, the advantage of the increased isolation which is necessary for the vine at 50° North more than compensates for the difficulty of working on such steep slopes.

Settlement and communications

Four villages lie along this section of the Rhine. In all cases, lack of flat land near the river has caused these settlements to assume a linear form. They are all located near to the point at which a tributary valley joins the Rhine, and usually the village has extended a short distance up the tributary valley. Settlements away from the Rhine show a complete contrast. The tributary valleys, at least in their lower parts, are far too narrow to allow space for villages. Settlements are therefore found on the plateau, and since relief is not such a controlling factor as along the banks of the Rhine, they tend to adopt a more compact shape. The dominance of the strongly nucleated form should be noted here. Study of the map extract shows remarkably few farms outside the villages. In the north-east a few hamlets and single buildings, prefixed by the word '*Siedlung*' (Settlement), lie away from the villages. These isolated settlements are of recent origin, and have generally been established since 1945 as a result of the influx of refugees from East Germany. High above the Rhine, and occasionally in tributary valleys, names with the suffix or prefix '*Burg*' are frequently seen. These are related to defensive positions and their associated castles. In earlier times the Rhine traffic was controlled by these fortresses and tolls exacted. Today they provide an attraction for tourists.

Both map and photograph indicate the importance of the Rhine as a routeway. The valley is served by two railways and two main roads, while the river obviously carries a great amount of barge traffic. It seems unlikely that such traffic is occasioned by the villages on the map extract, which show no evidence of industrial premises of any magnitude. The harbours at Oberwesel, south of St Goarhausen, and at St Goar show little, if any, development of buildings or premises. In fact these harbours serve as refugees for barges in times of flood. The Rhine is a routeway through the highland barrier between the industrialised regions on either side, the Ruhr and Cologne areas to the north and the cities of the Rhine Rift Valley (such as Karlsruhe, Mainz, Ludwigshafen and Mannheim) to the south. An indication of its significance and of the type of traffic can be seen in the following figures.

Goods traffic on the Rhine in Rheinland Pfalz 1965
(Rolandswerth in the north to Lingenfeld in the south)

Number of vessels	Goods traffic (in 1,000 metric tons)		
	Total	Outgoing	Incoming
66,614	33,270	16,994	16,276

Goods	Despatched (1,000 metric tons)	Entering (1,000 metric tons)
Plant and animal products	206·8	780·5
Cement and building materials	871·3	718·5
Stone, gravel, sand, chalk, etc.	13,536·3	6,811·0
Ore	377·2	366·7
Coal and coke	28·2	2,982·7
Oil and products	502·3	2,971·6
Chemical products	1,099·5	1,332·2
Iron and steel	304·6	178·6

Source: *Statistische Berichte*. Des Statistischen Landesamtes Rheinland-Pfalz, March, 1966.

Away from the Rhine, communications appear to be more difficult. There are no railways, but three 'A' class roads follow the narrow floors of tributary valleys. These ignore the considerable settlement on the plateau and appear to be part of the national road network. The plateau surface supports a dense network of local roads. These are often unmetalled, and mostly of a very minor character. Their purpose is a purely local one, serving land which is mainly under farm or wood. Connections between the plateau and the valley floor present difficulties. Most of these roads have a winding or zigzag section where they leave the Rhine or tributary valleys and ascend to the plateau.

Occupations

Map evidence for occupations is slender. The villages appear to be mainly concerned with agriculture and possibly forestry, although this latter occupation is likely to employ only small numbers. (Note the sawmill in the Hasenbachtal north of St Goarhausen.)

Along the Rhine there is some evidence of a tourist industry. The youth hostel near the Loreley, the camping-place south of St Goar and the many castles suggest a region that makes at least a part of its living from holiday-makers. Extractive industry is represented by a mine in the Volkenbachtal near Kaub, though there is no indication of the product. There is little evidence of processing and manufacturing industry, with the exception of one factory in the Bruchertal about 1 km from Kaub and the widespread milling industry. Mills appear to be the only buildings sited on the floors of some of the valleys. In the Forstbachtal, for example, four mills are to be found in a section of five km. One must beware of assuming these are working today. As in Britain, the once widespread milling industry has been largely concentrated in a smaller number of larger premises, and no longer relies on water power.

Village	Population at 31.12.64	Village	Population at 31.12.64	Village	Population at 31.12.64
Bornich	1,000	St Goarhausen	1,760	Dellhofen	349
Kaub	2,057	Patersberg	465	Biebernheim	672
Reichenberg	313	Oberwesel	3,628	Niederburg	614
Dörscheid	352	St Goar	2,099	Urbar	623

Source: Industrie—und Handelskammer Zu Koblenz.

The importance of the Rhine valley and its routeway is evident from these figures. Only Bornich of all the plateau villages reaches a population of 1,000.

The Kaub extract illustrates the geography of two worlds. The Rhine, with its barges carrying coal and oil, its railways and roads, its tourists and prosperous vineyards is very much a part of the busy commercial world of north-west Europe. A short distance away lies the contrasting world of the Taunus and Hunsrück Uplands, with life concentrated in quiet villages and concerned with farms and woods. The contrast is a consequence of isolation, an isolation brought about by the physical history of the region.

Exercises

1. The photograph is of the Loreley rock 2 kilometres south of St Goar. From which point is the photograph taken? Identify the features marked A–G on the photograph.
2. With the aid of sketch maps analyse the sites of the following villages: Bornich, Reichenberg, Oberwesel.
3. What conditions encourage the development of *(a)* strongly nucleated, and *(b)* dispersed forms of settlement?
4. How do you account for the rectilinear pattern of drainage shown on the map extract?
5. Attempt to relate the figures for goods received and exported by water from Rheinland-Pfalz to the location and types of industry found in the Land (Province).
6. How far is it true to say that the Hercynian Uplands of western Europe are repellent to cultivation and settlement?
7. Analyse the conditions under which the vine is cultivated in western Europe. Why are conditions so diverse? How is it possible for viticulture to survive in the more marginal areas?

Further reading

DICKINSON, R. E. *Germany. A General and Regional Geography*, Methuen 1953, chapter 17.
ELKINS, T. H. *Germany*, Chatto & Windus. 1968, chapter 14.
FEBVRE, L. and DEMANGEON, A. *Le Rhin*, Strasbourg, 1931.
MUTTON, A., *Central Europe*, Longmans, 1968, chapter 14.
YATES, E. M. 'The Development of the Rhine' *Trans. I.B.G.*, June, 1963.

Study 10
PLÖN
SCHLESWIG-HOLSTEIN
WEST GERMANY

A Landscape of Young Glacial Deposits.

Extract from Map Sheet L.1928. Plön. West German 1:50,000 Series. (M 745)

Published 1961.
Vertical interval of contours 10 metres.
(Form lines at 5 metre and 2.5 metre intervals on gentle slopes).

Reproduction by permission of Landesvermessungsamt, Schleswig-Holstein. Topographical map 1:50,000 sheet L1928.

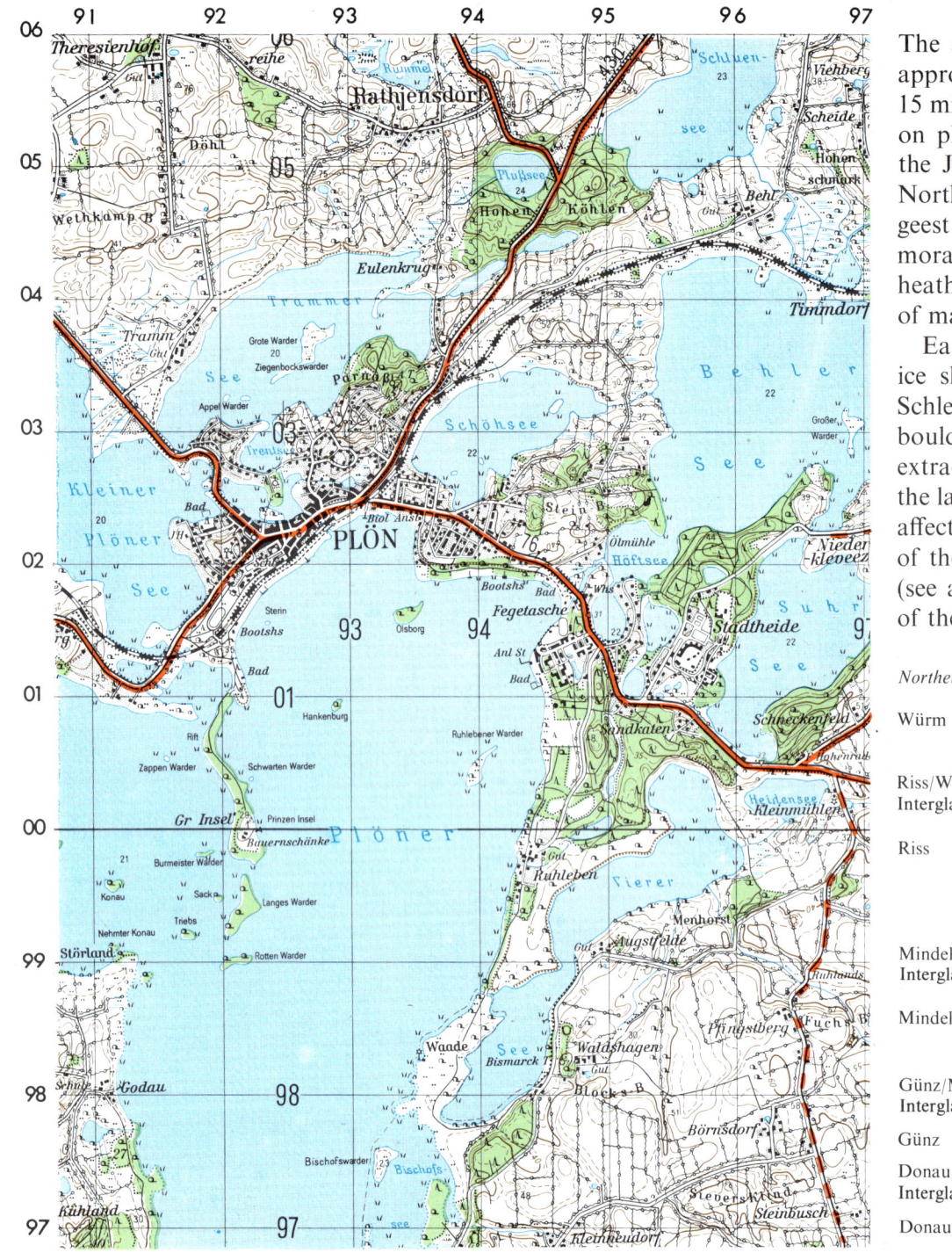

MAP 11

The area covered by the map extract is one of glacial deposition. It lies approximately midway between the Baltic ports of Kiel and Lübeck, about 15 miles distant from each. The Baltic coast is just visible in the far distance on photograph 13. Schleswig-Holstein, which forms the southern part of the Jutland Peninsula, can be divided into three contrasting sections: the North Sea coastlands with their fringe of marshes and mudflats, the sandy geest plateaux and fluvioglacial deposits of the central peninsula, and the moraines of the Weichsel or Vistula glaciation in the east. Thus the sandy heathlands of central Schleswig-Holstein separate relatively fertile districts of marine and glacial deposits to the west and east respectively (fig 15).

East of the River Elbe the intermittent northwards retreat of the Weichsel ice sheet is marked by a series of distinct moraines which converge in Schleswig-Holstein to form hills of up to 500 feet and between which are boulder clay plains and numerous lakes, as in the area covered by the map extract. Since these drift deposits of eastern Schleswig-Holstein relate to the last advance of the Scandinavian ice sheet, they have been relatively little affected by subsequent erosion compared with the sands of the central part of the peninsula, which were deposited during the earlier Saale glaciation (see also Study 11, Wolfsburg). The following table shows the glaciations of the North German Plain together with probable Alpine equivalents.

Northern Alps	North Germany	Remarks
Würm	Weichsel (Vistula)	Younger drift east of River Elbe. Three terminal moraines: North = Pomeranian; Central = Frankfurt; South = Brandenburg.
Riss/Würm Interglacial	Eem Interglacial	Marine and freshwater deposits.
Riss	Saale	Leached deposits west of River Elbe. Warthe terminal moraine is included here (Lüneburg Heath, Fläming, Lusatian Heath), although many geologists interpret it as the outermost stage of the Weichsel glaciation.
Mindel/Riss Interglacial	Holstein Interglacial	Marine and freshwater deposits.
Mindel	Elster	Scattered erratics along the northern edge of the Central Uplands of Germany.
Günz/Mindel Interglacial		No certain equivalent in North Germany. Deposits on the island of Sylt *may* represent a pre-Elster glaciation.
Günz		
Donau/Günz Interglacial		
Donau		

Photograph 13. Plön. Schleswig-Holstein.

Inter Nationes/Deutsche Luftbild KG, Bonn.

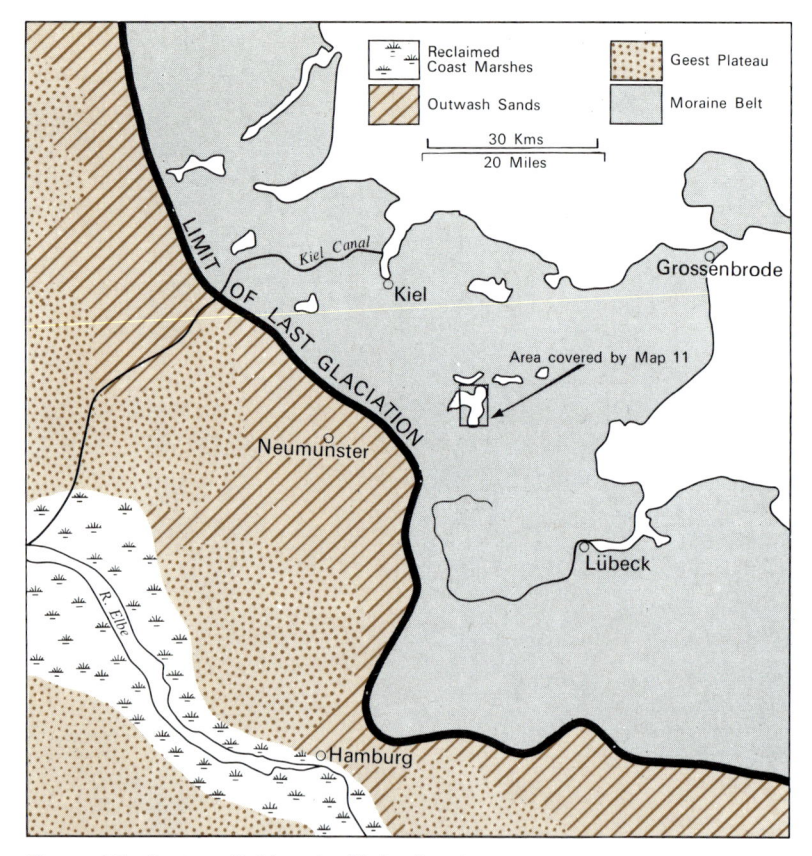

Figure 15. Eastern Schleswig-Holstein.

Relief and drainage of the Plön district

In describing the landforms developed on the Young Drift, R. E. Dickinson points out that 'the ground moraines were shifted about at the base of the Ice Sheet in various ways, so as to yield different kinds of surfaces when the ice retreated. Thus, there are ground-moraine plains *(Grundmoränenebene)* that form extensive level or gently undulating surfaces. Probably the ice was "dead" in these areas and gradually disappeared by melting rather than by movement of retreat. Hilly ground-moraine topography *(Kuppige Grundmoränenlandschaft)* has a maze of small steep-sided hills and hollows that often lack a normal drainage outlet and contain a lake or marsh. Such morainic deposits were formed at the edge of the Ice Sheet and merge into the terminal moraines'. Drumlins, eskers and melt-water channels are characteristic of this latter type of area.

The Plön district displays the typical features of the hilly ground moraine areas. The small hills are generally rounded and distributed in a confused, irregular manner. The hummocky nature of the ground is indicated by the alternation of embankments and cuttings along the main roads and railway. A very detailed picture of the relief can be built up from the map which has a vertical interval of as little as 2·5 metres on gentle slopes. The small hills and knolls are shown by closed contours, and, to facilitate interpretation, hollows, which are similarly indicated by closed contours, are marked by small brown arrows. The highest elevation is at 917056 where the ground rises 55 metres above Plöner See. The narrow, winding peninsula, Gross Insel, which projects into the lake south of Plön appears to be an esker, but a lack of further information makes a positive identification difficult.

Numerous lakes occupy the hollows between the hills. These depressions may have been formed by the slow melting of residual ice masses or by the blocking of valleys by moraines, or alternatively may have been cut by fluvioglacial streams. In other places pockets of low, badly drained ground give the impression of having been former lakes now infilled with sediment by the long continuation of the silting which appears evident around the margin of the present lakes. The map gives no information about the depth of the lakes, but the large number of small islands suggests that they are of no great depth, an impression borne out by photograph 13.

Land use

The soils of the Plön district are closely related to the glacial material from which they have developed. The ground moraine of the Weichsel glaciation has been far less leached than the Older Drift elsewhere and even brown earth soils are developed on the boulder clay in this area. These soils are heavy but fertile and are well suited to the needs of arable farming. They originally supported a cover of deciduous woodland with a predominance of beech, but little natural vegetation remains. In their natural state the depressions contain pockets of marsh, as at 945057, but in most cases artificial drainage channels are evident and many such hollows now contain meadows (912038) or a cover of trees and shrubs (967044).

The agricultural economy of eastern Schleswig-Holstein with its cool, moist climate is based upon mixed farming. On the arable land rye and oats are the chief cereal crops, although some wheat is grown. Rape-seeds and other oil seeds are sometimes grown as part of a long crop rotation practised in this area. A notable feature of the farming is the high proportion of land given over to cultivated grasses such as clover and lucerne. Thus there are close links between the arable farming and stock rearing. Large numbers of beef cattle, dairy cattle and pigs are kept in the region. Milk is sent to Kiel and Lübeck with which Plön is linked by the single track railway shown on the map. Hamburg too is sufficiently close to act as a market for milk. Large quantities of butter and cheese are also produced.

A striking feature is the division of the area into very small fields each enclosed by a 'low bank with hedge'. This pattern of plots is particularly evident in the south-east, where the fields tend to assume a series of narrow strips, as around the village of Kleinneudorf (946968) where the present field pattern no doubt reflects the former system of strip farming *(Gewanne)* which developed during the early Middle Ages.

Settlement

The settlement pattern of the area is dominated by the small township of Plön (population 9,800) which has grown up on an isthmus separating Plöner See from Kleine Plöner See and a number of other smaller lakes. It stands at the intersection of two main roads, route 76 (Lübeck/Kiel) and route 430 (Grossenbrode/Neumünster). The town stands at a height of 35 metres (14 metres above Plöner See) in the south, but rises to over 50 metres near the observation tower (A.T.) at Parnass in the north (934034). Apart from the central area, the town and its eastern extensions of Fegetasche (9401) and Stadtheide (9501) appear to be quite open in plan with many buildings and houses standing in spacious, wooded grounds often leading down to the shore of a lake. The low density of housing is borne out by an examination of photograph 13. The exact function of the settlement is difficult to determine from either the map or photograph. It is clearly an important nodal point in the local communications system and may be of some importance as a service centre for the surrounding agricultural communities. The presence of numerous small piers, a landing stage *(Anlegestation, abb. Anl.St.)*, boathouses *(Bootshs)*, together with numerous bathing beaches *(Bad)* on the lake shores suggests that sailing and swimming may be important tourist attractions and that Plön, with its pleasant wooded, lakeside site and old castle *(Schl)* attracts visitors from the nearby urban centres of north Germany.

The surrounding settlements are all very small. The largest, Rathjensdorf (9305), has less than 30 buildings and none of the hamlets in the area are of a sufficient size to include a church. All are situated on minor roads. An interesting aspect of the rural settlement is suggested by the term *Gut* which appears on the map extract at several points. The term *Gut* or *Gutshöfe* signifies a type of large estate which was formerly associated with the Junker landowners of the Mecklenburg and Brandenburg districts of East Germany. The appearance of the typical *Gut* is described by T. H. Elkins as follows: 'This was a world of its own ... with a group of very substantial farm buildings, including a manor house, extensive barns and byres and stables, houses for the labourers and often a distillery or similar enterprise for processing crops'. It can be seen from the extract that the pattern of small enclosed fields mentioned earlier is generally less evident in the vicinity of these estates than elsewhere. A typical example is that at Theresienhof (915057). This estate, which consists of a number of large buildings set around a yard, is approached from the south along a tree-lined avenue. Several cottages lie close to the estate while to the south of the main buildings is a large garden. Field sizes are larger here than elsewhere on the map.

The map provides little evidence of occupations. Foresters' cottages are shown at 965005 and 946052, and two watermills are marked, one on the small stream at Kleinmühlen (967002) and the other in the centre of Plön (927023) utilising the 1 metre difference in level between Plöner See and Trammer See. An oilmill *(Ölmühle)* located at 949022 may be used for the crushing of rape seed and other oil seeds grown locally. Even if still in operation these mills could provide employment for only small numbers. The map shows no evidence of manufacturing industry.

In the absence of industrial development it seems clear that the Plön district, with its fertile glacial deposits, is a typical area within the important mixed farming region of eastern Schleswig-Holstein, but possessing the additional advantage of a small tourist industry.

Exercises

1. What other information, apart from the map and photograph, would you require to make a positive identification of an esker south of Plön?
2. With the aid of diagrams, explain precisely the meaning of the following terms which occur in the study: *(a)* Leaching; *(b)* Brown Earth Soils; *(c)* Ground Moraine; *(d)* Esker; *(e)* Fluvioglacial deposit.
3. Give an explanatory account of the differences in the landscape of the Plön and Wolfsburg districts of the North German Plain. (See also Study 11.)
4. Why do the soils developed on glacial deposits in Europe vary in fertility? (O. & C.)

Further reading

DICKINSON, R. E. *Germany. A General and Regional Geography*, Methuen, 1953, chapters 2, 3, 9 and 24.
ELKINS, T. H. *Germany*, Chatto & Windus, 1968, chapter 17.
FLINT, R. F. *Glacial and Pleistocene Geology*, Wiley, 1957, chapter 23.
MUTTON, A. F. A. *Central Europe*, Longmans, 1968, chapter 16.
SINNHUBER, K. A. *Germany. Its Geography and Growth*, Murray, 1961.
WRIGHT, W. B. *The Quaternary Ice Age*, 2nd edn, Macmillan, 1937, chapter 10.

Study 11
WOLFSBURG
NIEDERSACHSEN
WEST GERMANY

An Area of Recent Industrial Development.

Extract from Map Sheet L.3530. Wolfsburg. West German 1:50,000 Series.

Published 1960.
Vertical interval of contours 10 metres.
(Form lines at 5 metre and 2.5 metre intervals on gentle slopes.)

Printed by permission of Niedersächsisches Landesverwaltungsamt of 28.11.67—B4-520/67. Reproduction in any form strictly prohibited.

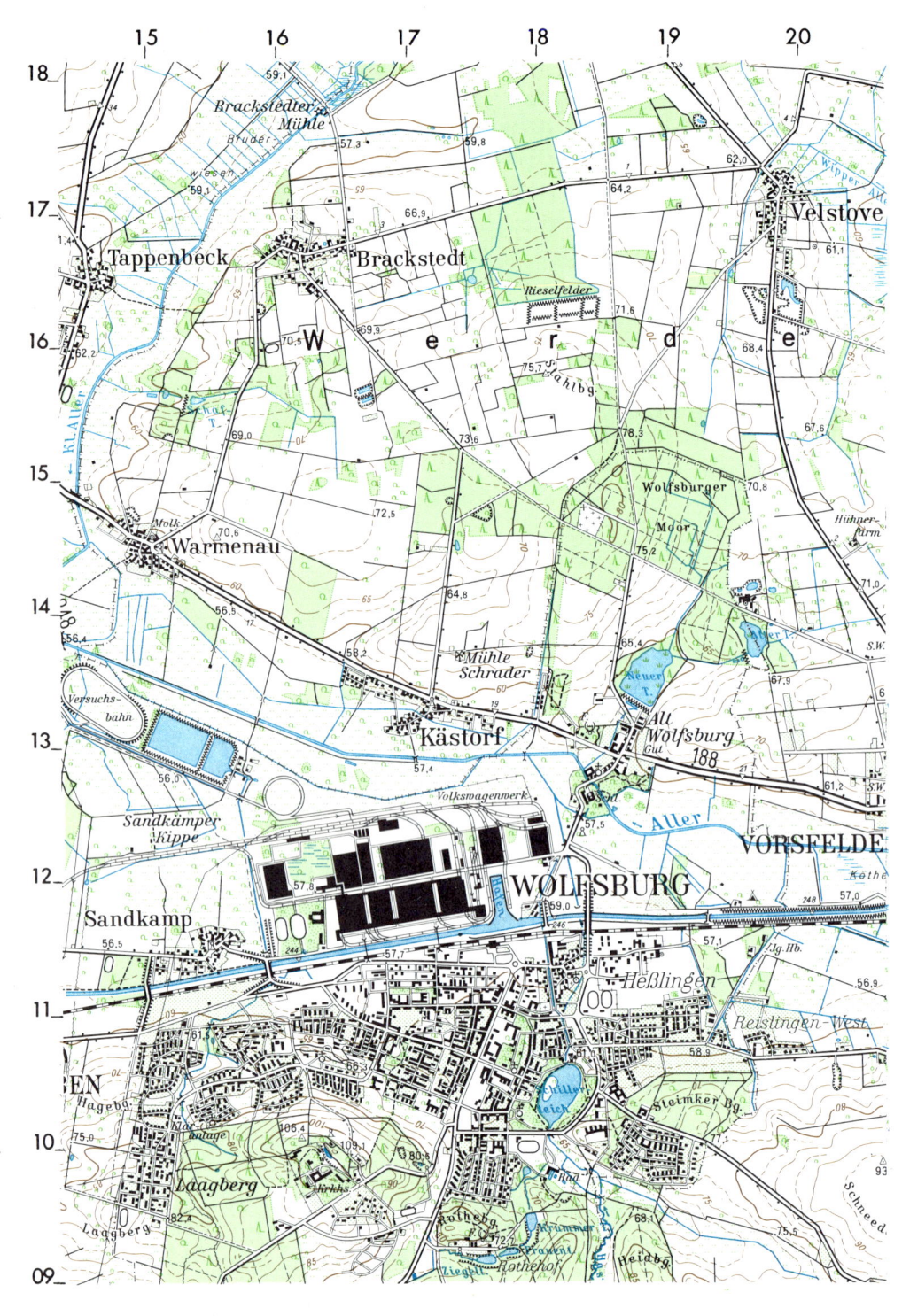

Map 12

Relief

The location map, fig. 16, shows that the map extract covers a small part of the North German Plain. The landscape can be divided into three contrasting units. To the north and south lie two upland areas, while across the centre of the map runs the lowland of the Aller with an extension to the north-west along its tributary the Kleine Aller. The greatest elevations are reached in the south, where spot heights of 106.4 metres and 109.1 metres are shown near the hospital (*Krkhs* 1609). The northern upland is generally lower, usually about 65 to 70 metres, but with a maximum of 80 metres on Wolfsburger Moor (1814). Summits are rather flat, but cut into them are a number of valleys. Some of these carry streams, others are dry, notably the one lying north of Kastorf (1613). Occasionally hollows with no outlet are found; such a depression is shown by Hühner Farm at 2014. The lowland areas of the Aller and Kleine Aller valleys lie between 56 and 60 metres above sea level. These are flat and many drainage ditches have been cut to lead excess water into the straightened rivers.

The origin of this landscape lies in the Quaternary glaciation. The uplands are composed of sands and gravels known as geest. The valley of the Aller was once a glacial meltwater channel. In fact, a hint of this is given by the great width of the valley compared with the rather small river which flows along it. This part of the North German Plain was not covered with ice during the last onset of the Scandinavian ice sheets (the Weichsel glaciation), although melt-water from this stage affected the region considerably by cutting great channels, or '*urstromtäler*' from the east to the North Sea. The sands and gravels were laid down in earlier advances of the ice, particularly during the Saale glaciation (see table in Study 10). Thus erosion has been at work for a relatively long period and many of the irregularities left after deposition have been removed. Areas of bog are also to be found among the geest deposits; note the area east of Velstove (2016).

Land use

The contrasts between uplands and lowlands are reflected in the pattern of land use. Although few symbols for types of cultivation are used on this series, the density of roads suggests that much of the upland country is farmland. In addition, there are large areas of woodland, much of it of the coniferous type which might be expected on sandy or gravelly soils. The photograph confirms these conclusions. The figures overleaf (1960) show the land use situation in the parishes of the extract, though unfortunately parish boundaries are not shown on this map.

Permanent grassland accounts for roughly one third of the farmland.

Photograph 14. The Volkswagen plant at Wolfsburg.

V.W. Press Information, London.

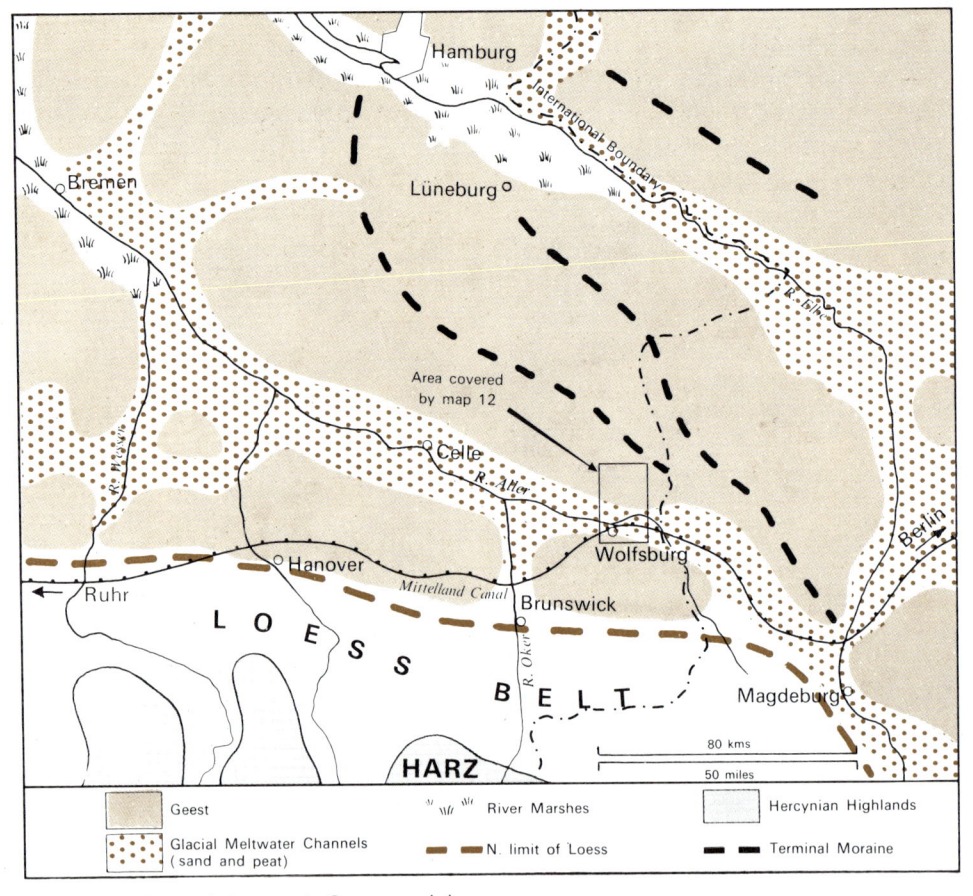

Figure 16. Part of the north German plain.

This consists of two types, meadow and heathland. The meadow lands lie mainly along the drained valley floors while the heathland is to be found on the geest plateau. The percentage of woodland varies widely, from 50% in Wolfsburg to less than 10% in Velstove and Sandkamp. The distribution of woodland seems to bear little relation to relief. Certainly the steeper slopes on Wolfsburger Moor are under woodland, but so also are large level stretches east of Brackstedt. It is likely that the soil factor is of the greater importance here; the poorer sands and gravels being left to woodland while the more fertile soils are cultivated. A surprisingly large proportion of the agricultural land is under the plough, always over 60% and around Brackstedt 71%. By far the most important crops are cereals, mainly rye and oats, and the balance is largely given over to root crops such as potatoes. Much of this land was originally of poor quality, in contrast to the fertility of the Börde country to the south. The modern pattern of cultivation is a result of clearance of heath and forest, and painstaking effort to improve the quality of largely podsolised soils with fertiliser.

The size of farms shows a wide range from less than half a hectare to over fifty hectares. The following is a breakdown of the 212 farm units in the parishes of the extract:

	Area of farms (in hectares)						
	0·01–0·5	0·5–2	2–5	5–7·5	7·5–10	10–20	20–50	Over 50
No. of farms	7	54	33	12	13	49	39	5

The majority of farm units are either very small or of moderate size, but unfortunately there is no evidence to suggest how these farms are distributed or the reasons for this variation. Considering the quality of the land it is doubtful whether the smallest holdings provide an adequate livelihood for a family.

Settlements

Settlement is very largely of a nucleated type; most people live in the villages or in Wolfsburg, few live in isolated farms. The sites of the villages are very similar; all of them are above the floodplains, none of them lies on the highest parts of the uplands. The heights of the villages vary between 57·5 metres (Sandkamp) and 67·5 metres (Brackstedt). All are therefore out of reach of floods, though presumably not far above the water table. The form of the villages is usually compact, though there is some extension along roads, notably in Kastorf which assumes the shape of a street village. Alt Wolfsburg seems to have grown up around a manor house *(Gut)* and castle *(Schloss)*. However, the photograph suggests that much new development has taken place around Alt Wolfsburg since the map was published. The form of Wolfsburg suggests a town of modern growth which has expanded in an east-west direction confined by the line of the Mittelland canal to the north and by steep wooded slopes to the south. The town gives an impres-

	Total land area in farm and forestry concerns in hectares	Forest land %	Agric. land %	Arable as % of agric.	Permt. grass as % of agric.	Cereals as % of arable	Hoed crops inc. sugar beet potatoes, turnips as % of arable
Tappenbeck	471	13	80	69	30	55	42
Brackstedt	565	12	80	71	26	58	42
Warmenau	508	11	87	67	32·5	52	47
Kästorf	391	14	82	69	29	56	43
Velstove	686	8	86	65	34	54	46
Sandkamp	287	5	91	63	35	62	38
Wolfsburg	905	50	41	67	36	75	22

Source: Niedersächsisches Landesverwaltungsamt, Statistik.

sion of a 'garden city' with its frequent open spaces. A notable feature is the number of large apartment blocks; both photograph and map show many of these, often arranged en echelon.

Occupations

Apart from the huge factory blocks of the Volkswagenwerk there is little direct evidence of occupations on the map. One may assume that most villages are concerned with agriculture, though the farm size figures suggest the possibility of labour surplus to farming requirements. Reference to the figures in Exercise 2 will show that Wolfsburg has a very large proportion of its workers in manufacturing industry (65%), the next most important categories being service occupations (over one sixth) and trade (over one tenth). The domination of the town by the Volkswagen (VW) factory is obvious, and several of the advantages of this location may be deduced.

Since the car industry is of recent growth, and space in the older industrial areas hard to find, the attraction of the flat floor of the Aller Valley must have been strong. Today, over two square miles are occupied by the VW plant and expansion appears to present few difficulties. Large areas are necessary not only for assembly lines, offices and power station, but also for the storage of completed vehicles awaiting export. North-west of the works lies a one and a half mile (2 km) long oval test track *(Versuchsbahn)* and adjoining it a large reservoir. The purpose of the latter is not clear; it may be related to the water requirements of the factory, to the needs of the town or even to the maintenance of water levels in the canal.

Communications are a second factor. The impressive network of railway lines within the works is linked in Fallersleben (1 km to the west) with the main line which runs east-west along the banks of the canal. Most raw materials, except for coal and oil, are handled by the railway, road transport being of far less importance. Ingots for the foundry, sheet metal, strip steel, castings, fabrics and upholstery, paints, lubricants and chemicals are brought to the works from suppliers in the Ruhr and Rhineland and from elsewhere within the Common Market. In return completed vehicles (5,700 produced each day) are carried to worldwide markets. The daily turnover of railway trucks is about 8,000.

The Mittelland canal is also of advantage in this location, providing a link with the coal-producing Ruhr and the seaports of Rotterdam, Bremen and Emden. To the east it is linked with the River Elbe and Berlin, a connection of little value in the present political situation. For the VW works the canal provides cheap transport for bulk cargoes of oil, coke and coal. In 1965 the power plant consumed 167,000 tons of oil and 284,000 tons of coal and coke. The photograph and map stress the significance of the canal with the power station and oil storage tanks lying next to the harbour.

A third factor in the growth of the works has been the supply of labour. The occupation tables in Exercise 2 for the surrounding villages and for Wolfsburg itself emphasize the importance of the factory. In fact about half of the employees commute daily from villages and towns up to a distance of 60 km. Being close to the frontier with East Germany (7 km to the east), the VW works have also benefited from the post-war influx of refugees. About 50% of the employees fall into this category. A second large group in the 47,000 employees is made up of Italians. Almost 5,000 work in the VW factory though most return home after a few years in Wolfsburg.

The 'garden city' appearance of Wolfsburg and the spaciousness of the factory site emphasize the advantages which modern industry has over the older sites usually so closely linked with coalfields (see Studies 6 and 7).

Exercises

1. Wolfsburg lies far from the sources of its raw materials and power. How then is the Volkswagen able to compete so effectively in world markets?
2. The following figures show the occupation structure of the settlements on the extract:

Settlement	Population	Working Population	Farming/ Forestry	Power and Water supplies	Manufacturing inds.	Building	Retail Wholesale and trade	Services and misc.
Wolfsburg	64,560	31,256	200	215	20,309	1,880	2,958	5,694
Sandkamp	661	337	41	—	163	79	23	31
Tappenbeck	638	299	68	1	156	27	21	27
Brackstedt	873	170	89	1	43	15	3	19
Kastorf	858	414	44	2	235	55	32	46
Velstove	415	210	104	—	60	25	5	16
Warmenau	352	196	98	1	48	16	11	22

Draw a sketch map of the area plotting communications and the 60-metre contour. Draw circles to represent each village proportionate in size to the working population. Divide the circles into segments to represent: *(a)* farming and forestry; *(b)* manufacturing industries; *(c)* other occupations. Comment on your resulting map.
3. Identify the view from the map. What developments have taken place since the map was published?
4. Explain the meaning of the terms: podsol, urstromtäler, geest, terminal moraine.
5. Why build large apartment blocks in a district with an apparent abundance of building sites?
6. Compare and contrast the value of inland waterways in Germany with those of Britain.
7. Under what conditions are marshes or bogs formed?

Further reading

DICKINSON, R. E. *Germany, A General and Regional Geography,* Methuen, 1953, chapter 19.
ELKINS, T. H. *Germany,* Chatto & Windus, 1968, chapters 2, 3 and 16.
ESTALL, R. C. and BUCHANAN, R. O. *Industrial Activity and Economic Geography,* Hutchinson, 1966.
SHACKLETON, M. R. *Europe,* Longmans, 1965, chapter 19.

Study 12
ROUEN
SEINE-MARITIME
FRANCE

A Bridge Point Settlement.

Extract from Map Sheets
XIX-11 Rouen Ouest and
XX-11 Rouen Est.
French 1:50,000 Series
(Type 1922)

Published 1955 and 1954.
Sheet XIX-11 Rouen Ouest
partially revised 1963.
Vertical interval of
contours 10 metres.
(Form lines at 5 metre
intervals on gentle slopes.)

Reproduced from maps published
by Institut Géographique
National, Paris.

66 Map 13

Photograph 15. The Seine at Rouen showing port and industrial developments.

Aerofilms Ltd., London.

The following five studies incorporate extracts from the French 1:50,000 and 1:25,000 series. Relief is expressed by contours and oblique hill shading on the 1:50,000 series. On this latter series contours are drawn at 10 metre intervals with an occasional 5 metre form line on gentle slopes, while on the 1:25,000 series the respective intervals are 5 metres and 2·5 metres.

Map 13 covers part of the Seine valley near Rouen. Although some 80 miles from the sea, the river lies only a few metres above sea level and a tidal influence is felt beyond Rouen. In spite of the river being so close to base level, the land on either side shows only a slight development of flood plains. These occur in the west (note the land below 10 metres west of St Martin de Boscherville), in the meander south of Rouen and in the lower part of the flat valley floor of the Cailly (west of Rouen). Elsewhere steep-sided plateaux occupy the greater part of the landscape. To the west of the Cailly valley and the Seine below Rouen lies the Forêt de Roumare reaching summit levels of over 100 metres. This is bounded by steep slopes (1 in 6) to the east and west. Its flat surface is dissected by several valleys, short and combe-like to the east, long and steep sided to the west. North and east of Rouen the plateau is dissected to form a number of steep sided, flat topped spurs.

This landscape suggests a surface which has been cut into by a rejuvenated drainage system. Comparison of plateau and river heights indicates incision to a depth of at least 100 metres. Obviously there must have been stages in this long process which may have left some traces in the form of river terraces. The area around le Génetey (0194) might suggest a level at about 80–90 metres. Similarly, contours and spot heights within Rouen and in the meander core to the south may provide evidence of lower terraces. Map evidence, however, is notoriously unreliable for these minor relief forms, especially when the contour interval is as great as 10 metres. J. Levainville, in his work on Rouen, distinguishes three terraces in the area. The highest of these is about 48 metres in the Forêt de Roumare and in the meander core south of Rouen; the second is at 25 metres in the meander core, while the third is at 10 metres above sea level. This latter terrace has been used as the site of Sotteville, Petit Quevilly, Grand Quevilly and St Martin de Boscherville.

Evidence of rock type is suggested by both map and photograph 15. The abundance of dry valleys, the steep but rounded slopes and the white rock exposures on the left of the photograph suggest chalk, although the dense woodland and patches of cultivation point to the existence of overlying superficial deposits. These may well be of limon, a fine grained, yellowish-brown loam dating from inter-glacial or post-glacial periods of steppe climate. Elsewhere the chalk is often hidden beneath deposits of clay-with-flints, thought to be a residual material formed from the weathering of chalk.

Settlement

Settlement in the area appears to be strongly influenced by relief. Along the western side of the Forêt de Roumare housing follows the roads near the foot of the slope. This ribbon of settlement extends southwards from les Sablons and reaches into the plateau only where tributary valleys allow, as at la Carrière and Quevillon. A second line of dwellings follows the bank of the Seine to the west leaving the floodplain devoid of farms or houses. It is likely that the river bank villages follow the crest of a protective embankment. A similar ribbon pattern follows the foot of the plateau slope in the east, from Croisset to Quenneport. In contrast to the riverine settlement, plateau villages tend to assume a more compact form, often with patches of cultivated land included in the village. Part of Canteleu is visible in the photograph and the large blocks suggest that this village is within the residential zone of Rouen.

The core of Rouen lies north of the Seine in the vicinity of the Palais de Justice. The advantage of this site lies in its proximity to the bridges across the Seine at the former lowest bridging point. Furthermore the low terraces mentioned previously provide a site free from severe flooding. Extension from the central area has come only with considerable human effort in the clearance of forest, the drainage of marshes, the embankment of the river, and above all the establishment of a fast and efficient communication system surmounting the steep slopes which almost surround the town. Today housing spreads even across the steep edges of the plateau to the north, and separate villages such as les Cottes now form suburbs. In the neighbourhood of Mt Fortin buildings are found on slopes of 1 in 5, though streets tend to run along rather than against the slopes. South of the river relief has had less influence. The city has grown in a radial manner from the Seine bridges, engulfing the older nucleii of the villages of le Petit Quevilly, le Grand Quevilly and Sotteville. Both the layout and the nomenclature of certain of these developments indicate very recent growth. In the south occur Cité 4, Cité 3 and le Grd Quevilly Ext^{on}, while along the road south of le Grand Quevilly, but off the extract, lie Cité Sonopa, Cité des Potasses and Cité Shell Berre. These are apparently carefully planned housing projects for workers, provided by industrial or municipal authorities.

Rouen lies 80 miles from the sea and 150 river miles from Paris, at the point where river- and sea-borne traffic meet. Although prosperous in the

Middle Ages, by the mid-nineteenth century Rouen found itself at a disadvantage compared with le Havre. Problems of the increasing size of ships and the difficult nature of the river channel were only solved by a programme of river improvement and dock construction after 1848. Today the sea port extends on both banks of the river for 19 km below the Boïeldieu Bridge (100937) while the river port reaches 13 km upstream to Oissel. Traffic through the port is immense and reached a total of over 10 million metric tons in 1965. The port tends to specialise in importing bulky goods of relatively low value and consequently the import tonnage is vastly greater than that exported. Various parts of the port specialise in different commodities. On the Rollet Peninsula at 078943 lies the coal port, in the basin south of it the timber dock, while the St Gervais basin handles wines and general cargoes. Upstream beyond the Boïeldieu Bridge lies the river port. This is of considerable importance, with its connections not only to Paris but also to parts of Lorraine and eastern France. Barge traffic supplies 30% of Rouen's exports and disposes of 70% of her imports. It is obvious from the map and photograph that the railway system is well integrated with the needs of the port. The chief marshalling yards are at Sotteville, which is the third most important railway junction in France.

Analysis of photograph and map gives much information about the industrial activity of Rouen. Perhaps the best known branch is that of textiles. This originated in the farms of the area as a woollen industry, but later passed through a linen stage until in the 18th century cotton became the chief interest. The transition to a factory industry was brought about by the use of large machinery, and led to a concentration in the valleys adjacent to Rouen, where water power, imported cotton and later coal (for steam power) were easily available. On the map several factories (Us^{es}) are marked in the Cailly valley (referred to by Levainville as 'la Petite Vallée de Manchester'). In fact there are over 40 establishments today producing not only cottons but also rayon, nylon and woollen goods, both near and in Rouen itself.

A considerable development of other industries has occurred as a result of the port's activities. Oil is imported (mainly by pipe line from le Havre) and processed in three large refineries belonging to Shell, Esso Standard and Socony Vacuum. The map and photograph show many oil storage tanks in le Petit Quevilly, though the major refineries are further downstream. Two of the paper factories shown produce over 50% of the newsprint required by the French press (note the abbreviation Pap^{ie} in Croisset and le Grand Quevilly). Chemicals and metals are two further industries mainly dependent on imported commodities, and in a similar manner are located close to the river in the maritime port (*Hauts Fourneaux,* abb. H^{ts} F^{neaux} = blast furnaces).

With its judicious blend of commercial and manufacturing activities Rouen provides an excellent example of a settlement which has achieved success through the intelligent adaptation of its site. Though this has presented difficulties, notably those of flood and communications, the position at a key bridging point and on a major routeway to Paris has proved of overriding significance in its development as a major port and city.

Exercises

1. Attempt to construct a map showing the distribution of industrial premises in Rouen on a tracing of the extract. What conclusions can you draw from this distribution?
2. The following figures refer to agriculture in two communes:

	No. of farms	Arable lands Total	Cereals	Pasturelands	Vines	Market gardens
		(expressed as a percentage of farm area)				
St Martin de Boscherville	60	17	10	82	—	0·3
Montigny	22	44	27	55	—	1

Source: *Recensement Général de l'Agriculture* 1956.

		Numbers of Animals			
	Horses	Cattle including	Dairy cows	Sheep	Pigs
St Martin de Boscherville	33	583	285	19	9
Montigny	14	145	70	4	13

Source: *Recensement Général de l'Agriculture* 1956.

Comment on the contrasts revealed by these figures.

3. How far can the map explain the distribution of woodland in the area?
4. Write an essay on the relative significance of inland waterway communications in France and Germany.
5. Assuming you could visit Rouen, how would you substantiate Levainville's identification of three levels of terraces in the area?
6. By what criteria do you judge the site of a port?
7. Compare the influence of relief on the patterns of growth and development of communications in Rouen and Liège (Study 6).
8. Describe the distribution of the French textile industries. What parallels and contrasts are there with those of Britain?

Further reading

France, Vol IV Naval Intelligence Geographical Handbook Series, 1942.
LEVAINVILLE, J. *Rouen,* Armand Colin, 1913.
MONKHOUSE, F. J. *A Regional Geography of Western Europe,* Longmans, 1965, chapter 9.
ORMSBY, H. *France,* Methuen, 1950, chapter 4.
POUNDS, N. J. G. 'Port and Outport in North-west Europe', *The Geographical Journal.* Vol. CIX. nos 4–6, October, 1947.

Study 13
CARCASSONNE
AUDE
FRANCE

An Historic Town of the Midi.

Extract from map sheets 5-6 and 7-8 Carcassonne French 1:25,000 Series.

Published 1958.
Vertical interval of contours 5 metres.
(Form lines at 2.5 metre intervals on gentle slopes).

Reproduced from maps published by Institut Géographique National, Paris.

Map 14

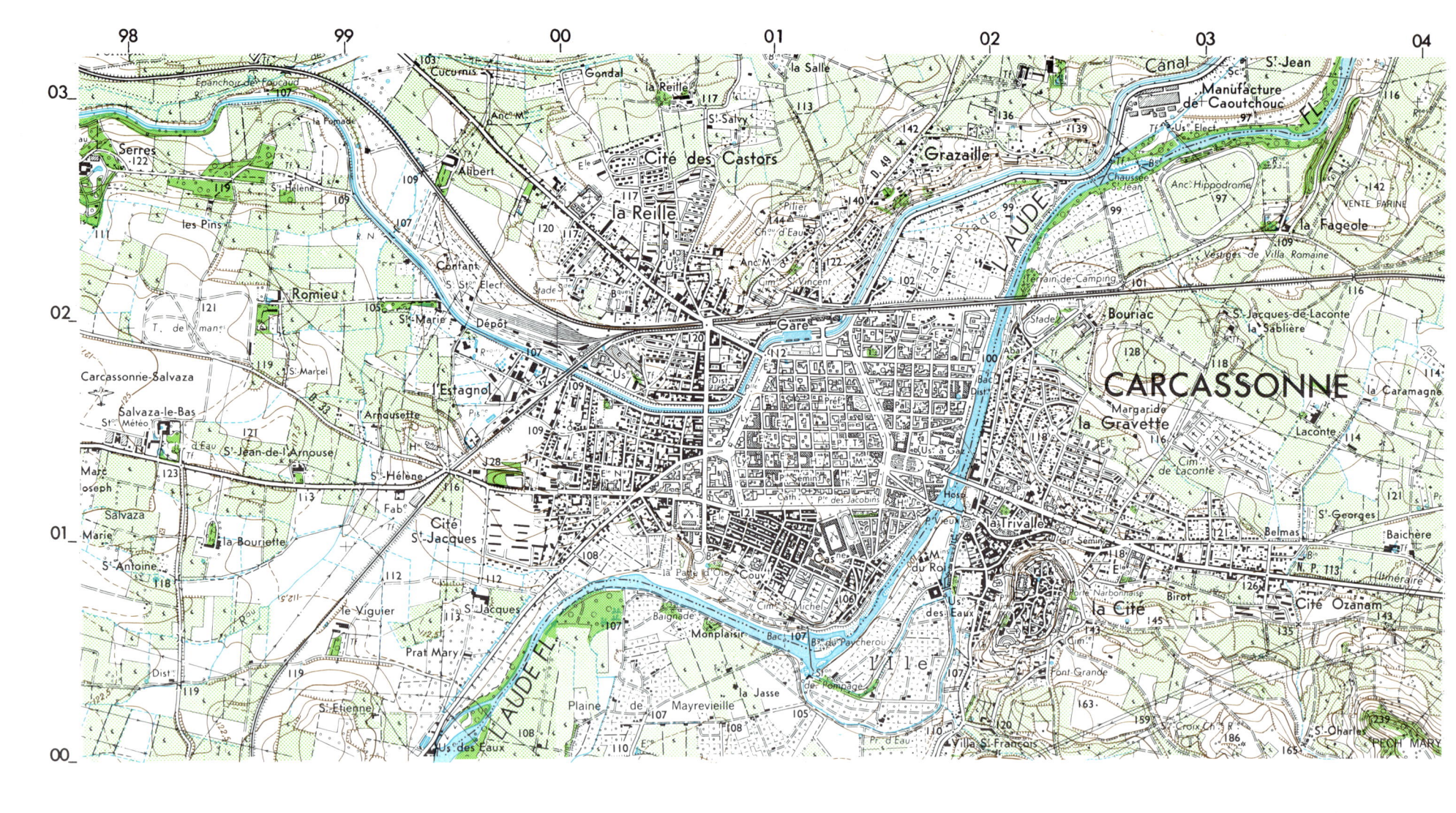

The map extract of Carcassonne provides an example of the French 1:25,000 map series, and it is interesting to compare the cartographic style with that of the Ordnance Survey 2½ inch:1 mile series which is drawn at the same scale. The extract shows part of the Carcassonne Gap which constitutes an important routeway between the Mediterranean coast and the Aquitaine Basin of western France. In this area the River Aude emerges from the Pyrenees and is joined by the River Fresquel before turning east to follow the direction of its tributary. Fig. 17 shows that the Col de Naurouze carries routes from the valley of the upper Fresquel to Toulouse and the Basin of Aquitaine beyond. On the map extract the Toulouse-Narbonne road (Route Nationale 113) is seen to pass through the town together with the main railway and the Canal du Midi. The latter, opened in 1680, in fact now carries only a very small local traffic in wine, casks and farm produce, on account of its inadequate width and depth (5½ feet). A branch road and single track railway lead south from the town to Perpignan via Quillan.

Relief and drainage of the Carcassonne district
The map area is one of varied relief bordering the valley of the River Aude. The land to the north of the river is generally gently undulating but culminates in a narrow ridge which attains heights of over 140 metres in the

Photograph 16. Carcassonne showing the 'Cité' and the Ville Basse in the background.

Photo Reportage YAN, Toulouse.

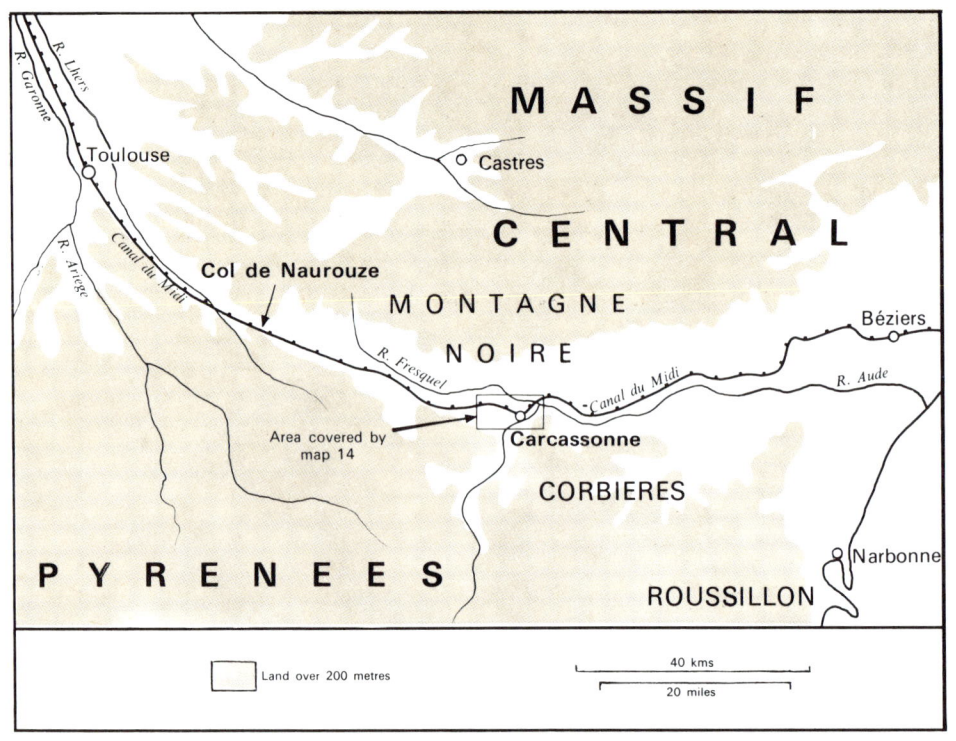

Figure 17. The Carcassonne gap.

Grazaille district to the north of Carcassonne. The section of ground between the Canal du Midi and the Aude which is occupied by the central area of Carcassonne shows a notable flattening and gives every indication of being a fragment of a river terrace. In the west the land rises gently to heights of over 125 metres in the vicinity of Carcassonne-Salvaza aerodrome. South of the river the relief is more striking. Much lies above 125 metres. In the extreme south-east a ridge of higher and more dissected ground reaches a maximum height of 239 metres at Pech Mary. This ridge terminates in a small but steep-sided hill of over 150 metres which overlooks the Aude and is occupied by the *cité* of Carcassonne.

The River Aude attains a width of about 80 metres to the south of Carcassonne and in the section covered by the map extract has an average gradient of *c.* 1 in 350. However, the presence of weirs along its course (*Barrage,* abb. *Bge.* = a weir) suggests an irregular long profile. The existence of sand banks in the river and shingle banks along its margin indicates considerable deposition despite the quite steep fall of the river, a situation which probably results from marked seasonal fluctuations of level of the river. The tributary channel in the Ile district to the south of Carcassonne suggests the abandonment of an earlier course. Away from the main river there is little surface drainage. To the west of the town a small stream (*Ruisseau,* abb. *Rau* = a stream) flows northwards under the canal, but most stream courses are temporary or dried up (the broken blue lines). The presence of numerous wells, water towers and sluices suggests an area in which a lack of water and the conservation and careful utilisation of existing resources are prime considerations.

The urban morphology of Carcassonne

In his book *The West European City* R. E. Dickinson points out that 'Carcassonne illustrates the features that typify the towns of the Midi. The oldest settlement, the *cité,* was a fortress on a hilltop, defended by walls and a castle and containing a very irregular street plan; here too were the homes of the lesser nobility. The *ville basse* lies on the opposite bank of the Aude river with a rectilinear plan and a central square market place, characteristic of the founded *bastides*'.

As can be seen from the map extract and photograph 16, the *cité* was a relatively small, compact settlement within double turretted ramparts with two entrances, the Porte Narbonnaise and the Porte d'Aude. The hilltop site stands about 50 metres above the level of the Aude and the surrounding slopes are very steep, especially on the western side where they exceed 1 in 2. Around the foot of the hill a number of wells and a spring may be noted in addition to a small reservoir within the walls of the *cité* itself. It is clear that ease of defence together with commanding views of the surrounding countryside, availability of water supply, elevation above the level of river floods, possibilities of cultivation on the sunny south-facing side of the ridge and the proximity of the important trade route through the Carcassonne Gap all motivated the original choice of site for the settlement. The *château* shown within the walls of the *cité* actually occupies the site of a Gallo-Roman *castellum.* Remains of a Roman villa are also shown to the north of the *cité* (033024). The Gallic city of Carcasso was occupied by the Visigoths in the 5th to 8th centuries and by the Saracens in the 8th century. However, it was not until the 12th century that Carcassonne rose to a position of importance in southern France and began to dominate the surrounding region.

Following the destruction of the dwellings outside the city walls during a siege in 1240 a new settlement was founded in 1247 on the opposite bank of the Aude. This was the *ville basse* with its rectilinear pattern of streets. It is apparent that expansion from the original nucleus of the settlement did not proceed in the normal manner by a gradual extension of buildings and streets, but by the complete transference of the urban centre to the opposite bank of the river. The *ville basse* and *cité* were linked by the Pont Vieux in the 13th century. In the case of the *cité* its strategic importance finally declined after 1659 when the Rousillon district was annexed to France. The *cité* in fact fell into a period of complete decline and much of the stonework was used to construct new buildings beyond the original walls.

The most immediately striking feature of the urban plan of Carcassonne is the symmetry of the street pattern of the *ville basse*, a clear example of planned rather than natural growth. Many towns in south-west France were founded during the Hundred Years War between England and France (1338–1453). These *bastides* (a Provençal word meaning fortress) were established as fortified trading centres, and many display a regular rectangular plan with a central market place and equally spaced streets, as in the case of Carcassonne. This medieval planning device was repeated many times in the region with varying degrees of modification according to the controls of site. The central *ville basse* now contains the principal public and institutional buildings of the city including the town hall *(Hôtel de Ville)*, law courts *(Palais de Justice)*, préfecture, markets, cathedral, etc.

The subsequent growth of Carcassonne has generally been characterised by an unplanned, piecemeal expansion of the town beyond the limits of the *bastide*, particularly along the Toulouse-Narbonne road as at la Reille and la Trivalle. These districts, like the areas to the south and west of the central area, are chiefly residential in function. Housing areas of a different type are represented by Cité des Castors, Cité St Jacques and Cité Ozanam, all on the edge of the town. These constitute the newest housing in Carcassonne and consist of blocks of flats arranged in an open and informal plan.

The extract shows only limited amounts of industry in and around Carcassonne. From the 12th century until the 19th century the district was important as a centre of textile manufacturing, but the industry declined with the rise of modern mechanised textile industries in northern France and elsewhere. However, the industries of the city are at present undergoing a revival following the development of Pyreneean hydro-electric power sites, as, for example, along the upper Aude. The chief industries at the present time include rubber production (the factory at St. Jean to the north-east of the town employs 600 workers), distilling, food industries and the production of farm machinery. The town also plays an important part in the wine trade of the region and is the collection and distribution centre for wine from the surrounding district.

It is clear that the present urban form of Carcassonne (population 43,000) is the product of a complex interaction of both geographical and historical influences. Factors which appear to have been particularly important include the configuration of the site, the planning ideas which prevailed during the growth of the town and changes in its function. As R. E. Dickinson points out, 'as in the field of geomorphology, the geographical study of urban, as of rural, settlements has three aspects. There is the physical "structure" of the settlement—the mode of grouping of its buildings and streets; there is the "process" which determines this structure—the social and economic character of the community; and third, there is the "stage" in the historical development of the settlement.'

Exercises

1. What are the essential characteristics of the 'Midi'? Where would you place the limits of the 'Midi'?
2. How far is it true to say that the growth of towns is the result of geographical factors? (O. & C.)
3. With reference to a selection of *Bastide* towns in southern France, show how the same planning device was repeated with only limited modifications.
4. Draw a cross section through Carcassonne to illustrate the main elements of the site. Label the physical features and districts of the town crossed by your section.
5. By reference to the map extract and the figures given below, write an explanatory account of land use in the Carcassonne district.

Commune of Carcassonne. Aude. Agricultural Statistics 1965

Land Use (in hectares)		Livestock			
Vines	3,108	Horses	294	Number of farms	625
Cereals	1,281	Sheep	181	Number of	
Roots	664	Pigs	75	agricultural workers	1,055
Market gardens, Orchards	220	Cattle	39	Number of tractors	294
Grassland	49				
Other land uses(¹)	1,524	(¹) Woodlands, Wasteland and built-up area.			
Total	6,846				

Source: *Recensement Général de l'Agriculture*, 1965. Inventaire Communal.

Further reading

CHABOT, G. *Les Villes*, Armand Colin, Paris, 1948.
DICKINSON, R. E. 'Le Développement et la Distribution du Plan Mediéval en Echiquier dans le Sud de la France et l'Est de l'Allemagne,' *La Vie Urbaine* **47**, 1938.
DICKINSON, R. E. *The West European City*, 2nd edn, Routledge and Kegan Paul, 1961.
LEVEDAN, P. *Géographie des Villes*, Paris, 1936.
MUMFORD, L. *The Culture of Cities*, 3rd edn, Secker and Warburg, 1958.
SMAILES, A. E. *The Geography of Towns*, Hutchinson, 1953.

Glossary of terms and abbreviations used on the map extract

$Anc.^n\ M.^{in}$—*ancien moulin* Disused mill
Bac.—Ferry
$B.^{in}$—*basin* Reservoir
$Cas.^{ne}$—*caserne* Barracks
$Ch.^{au}\ d'Eau$—*château d'eau* Water-tower
$Dist.^{le}$—*distillerie* Distillery
$E.^{le}$—*école* School
Épanchoir—Canal regulator
$Fab.^e$—*fabrique* Factory
$P.^{lle}$—*passerelle* Footbridge
Pr.d'Eau—*prise d'eau* Canal regulator; sluice
$Us.^e$—*usine* Factory

Study 14
SOLLIÈS-PONT
PROVENCE
FRANCE

A Provençal Landscape.

Extract from Map Sheet XXXIII-46. Toulon. French 1:50,000 Series.

Published 1935. Partial Revision 1958. Vertical interval of contours 10 metres.

Reproduced from a map published by Institut Géographique National, Paris.

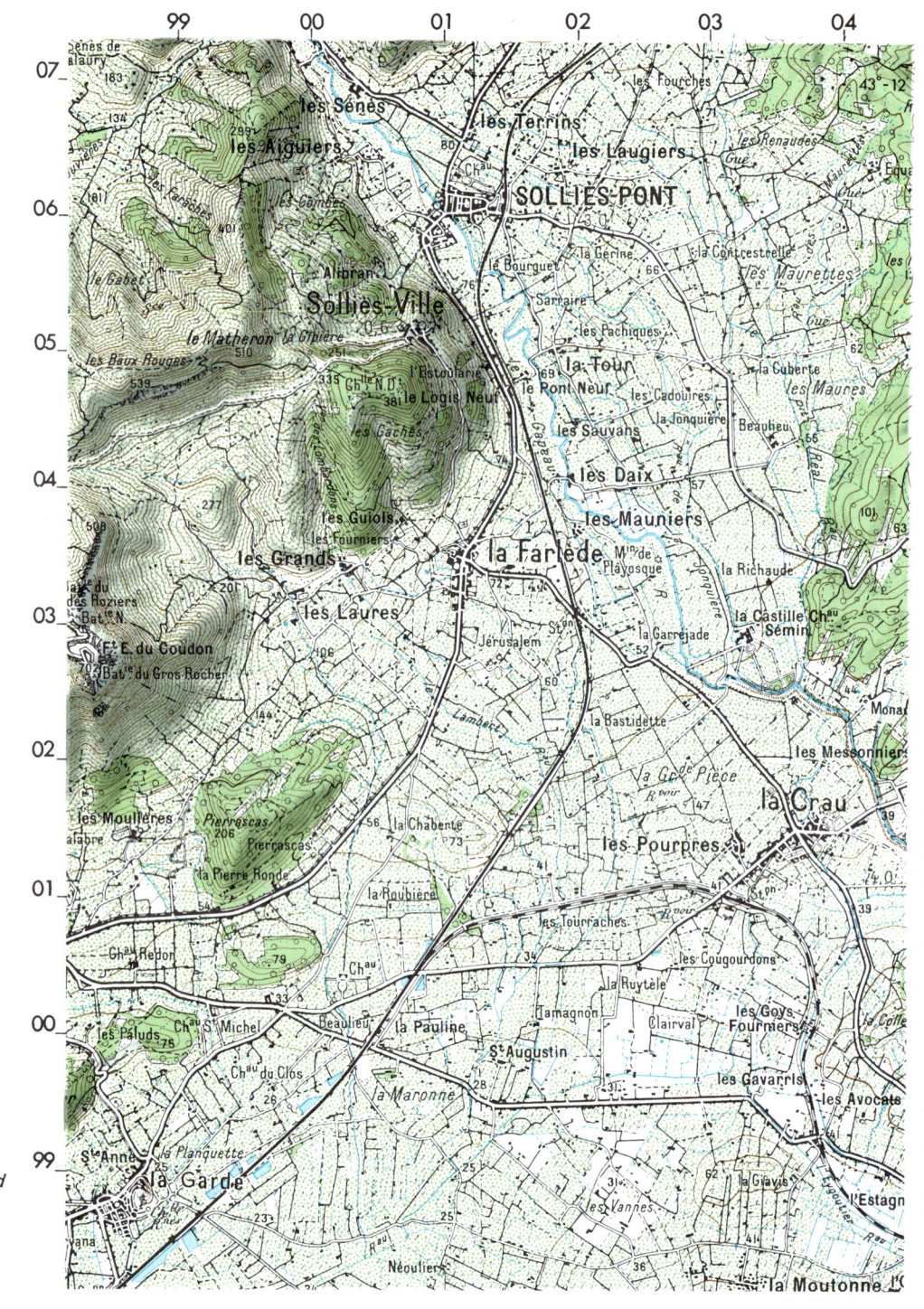

Map 15

Photograph 17. Solliès Pont. Plain of the Gapeau.
Aerofilms Ltd., London.

The location of the map extract is shown in fig 18. To the north and northwest lie the most southerly of the Alpine chains; to the east lie the Massifs of Les Maures and L'Esterel. Between the two, the map shows part of the plain of Hyères, one of the largest areas of lowland on the French Mediterranean coast east of Marseilles.

Relief and drainage

The landscape shown on the map and photograph falls naturally into two types, hills and plain. The plain slopes gently from 70 to 80 metres in the north to under 30 metres in the south. The relief of the plain is diversified by several knolls, notably at 0101 and 0398. On either side there is a gentle rise to the foot of the hills, then a marked break of slope where the steep-sided uplands are reached. The hills reach their greatest height and are at their steepest (1 in 3) in the west (Massif du Coudon 702 metres). Several steep-sided valleys dissect the hills and the upland is often thereby reduced to a series of ridges. In the south-west, erosion appears to have led to the severance of several outliers from the main hill mass. In the east less of the upland area is shown on the extract and slopes are less steep (1 in 10), but a number of short valleys appear to cut into the hills.

Over much of the plain, drainage is artificially directed. The main stream is the Gapeau which runs south-east close to La Crau. A low watershed separates the Gapeau basin from that of the Eygoutier which drains the southern area. The western hills show no evidence of permanent drainage except in the deep valley in the extreme north. In several cases valleys are completely dry, in others a seasonal flow may be assumed from the pecked blue lines. The eastern hills appear to be better watered, though even here streams are ephemeral. From the evidence of the dry valleys, the extremely steep slopes (notably near Les Baux Rouges at 9805, and the Massif du Coudon), and the general absence of any vegetation cover more luxuriant than brushwood, one can assume that the western highlands are probably composed of limestone. The eastern hills, with their less arid and rocky slopes covered with a much denser woodland, appear to be formed of a less permeable, though still resistant, rock.

The location map shows that the plain is part of a broad depression separating the limestones of the Provence Alps behind Toulon and Marseilles from the older crystalline highlands which reach the coast between Toulon and Cannes.

Land use

Both the map and photograph show a marked contrast in land usage between the hill country and the plain.

The hill masses of Le Coudon and Le Matheron (9905) appear to be of little agricultural use. The steep slopes (often reaching gradients of 1 in 3 or more), the absence of water and the presence of a poor brushwood vegetation *(garrigue)* over the greater part offer difficulties to arable cultivation. Reference to the photograph will substantiate these conclusions. Indeed, these hills appear to be only fit for the sheep or the goat to graze. In the lower parts of the two valleys which dissect this hill mass, the symbol for meadow or grassland is shown, together with a considerable number of

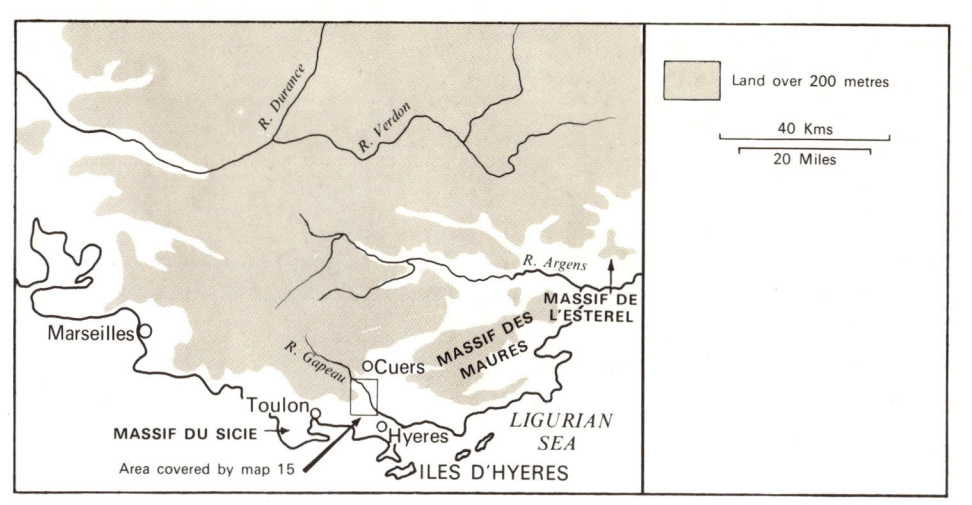

Figure 18. Provence.

buildings connected by footpaths. One may assume that these are farms, though it is doubtful if their standard of living is very high in such difficult surroundings.

The eastern hill masses, together with the three isolated knolls in the south-west, are almost devoid of settlement.

The plain is a different world. Slopes are gentle, water seems plentiful, and no doubt soils are of a thickness and fertility unknown in the hills. The map gives a fair amount of information about land use. Over a great part of the region the vine is dominant, but it is frequently associated with the growth of fruit trees. Orchards without vines occur in a discontinuous belt along the gently sloping land at the foot of the western hills and along either side of the Gapeau River between Les Sénès (0006) and Les Mauniers (0103). The most notable absence is that of land devoted to arable cultivation for cereals or similar field crops.

Fig. 20 is based on studies issued by the agricultural authorities for the Department of Var, and shows the situation in the neighbourhood of Solliès Pont in greater detail than on the topographical map. The boundary of the region surveyed coincides with the edge of the steep slopes of the hill masses (about 150 metres in the west and 100 metres in the east). On the south it follows the boundary between the communes of Solliès Ville and La Farlède. The figures stress the importance of fruit and the vine. Either on their own or with the vine, fruit trees cover 57% of this low-lying land. The evidence of the topographical map concerning the lack of arable cultivation is also confirmed; only 28 hectares (4%) are given to cereals and

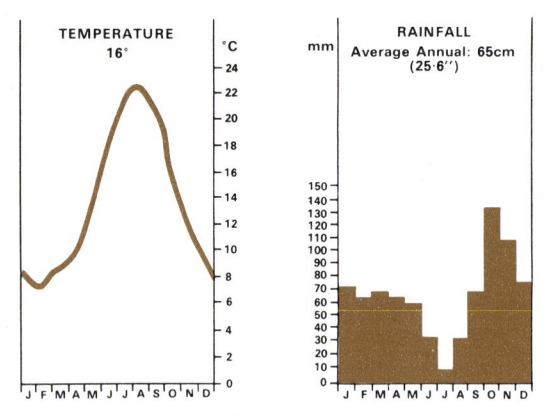

Figure 19. Climate graphs for Cuers. Provence.

fodder.

The reasons for this pattern of land use are partly revealed by the map extract. The inference of thick, fertile, possibly alluvial soils has already been made, but a study of the watercourses shows an additional reason for their fertility. The Gapeau is a permanent stream and feeds many small canals from two main points, one just south of Les Sénès, the other west of La Tour. The eastern part of the region is insufficiently irrigated largely because its watercourse, le Petit Réal, carries little volume compared with the Gapeau. It is significant that this area is largely given over to the vine, a plant which survives happily with little water. A third important factor is not revealed by the map. This is climatic. Graphs from the nearest recording station, at Cuers, indicate some important advantages, particularly for fruit and market garden produce. The warm springs, the hot summers and the absence of really low temperatures are all significant. The insolation figure for Cuers is 2,882 hours and for Toulon 2,915 hours. (Eastbourne on the coast of Sussex experiences 1,809 hours per year.) Thus the area is one of the most favoured in France—the problems are mainly those of water supply in the dry summer months. Paradoxically an additional problem of excess water occurs in spring and autumn when rain-storms frequently produce floods on the plain, particularly east of La Garde, where the Eygoutier stream normally floods 800 hectares of land each year. A fourth factor in the development of this fruit and vegetable economy is the existence of transport facilities to the great markets in Paris and Lyons. Thus the traditional Mediterranean pattern of farming involving cereal, olive, vine and sheep or goats has been superseded by a far more specialised type.

The following figures refer to size of farms and fields in relation to crops in the section of the plain delimited in fig. 20.

Size of farm (in ha.)	No. of farms	Total areas of farms (in ha.)	% of total area	Fields No.	Av. size (in ha.)	Use of land Waste or Fallow	Vines	Veg.	Orchard and orchard with vines	Cereals and fodder
Under 2	163	127	17	236	0·5	19	47	11	46	4·2
2– 4·99	55	174	25	97	1·8	24	29	7·6	107	6·3
5–13·99	33	226	31	61	3·7	2	18	0·2	195	11
Over 14	7	193	27	20	9·7	50	57	21	58	7
	Total 258	Total 720		Total 414	1·7	95	151	40	406	28

Source: Société du Canal de Provence et d'Aménagement de la Région Provençale. Étude Générale des Régions Desservies. Secteur 14. Solliès-Pont.

63% of the farms are of less than 2 hectares and generally consist of small fields (average ½ hectare in size). Upon these farms the vine is the dominant crop. Fruit production seems to be of the greatest importance on farms of moderate size (2–14 hectares), and the size of fields shows a marked increase to an average of 2 hectares or more.

The labour situation upon these farms is of interest.

Size of farm (in ha.)	No. of farms	Family Working on farm	Working off farm	No. of employees	Density per farm
Under 2	163	244	93	4	1·5
2– 4·99	55	73	19	12	1·5
5–13·99	33	62	3	16	2·4
Over 14	7	24	0	64	12

Source: Société du Canal de Provence et d'Aménagement de la Région Provençale. Étude Générale des Régions Desservies. Secteur 14. Solliès-Pont.

The small farms are obviously not capable of supporting the families who live on them. Thus almost one person in two travels outside the farm to work, possibly in the local town or even further afield, in Toulon.

The origin of the problems of small fields and small farms lies in such factors as the traditional French inheritance laws. This, together with the piecemeal buying of small patches of land, leads to fragmentation or *morcellement*. With an intensive type of agriculture producing fruit and vegetables the problem seems less acute than in other parts of France, where cereals and livestock are of greater importance and larger fields more economical.

The pattern of farming in the more southerly part of the plain appears to be similar to the north. The following statistics refer to the commune of La Farlède, the boundary of which may be traced on the map. Unlike the area of fig. 20, this commune includes both plain and hill country.

Crop production (areas in hectares)

No. of farms	Cereals	Arable land	Meadow/permanent grass	Vines and orchards	Market gardens veg. and flowers	Total area
156	2	20	11	245	73	446

Livestock (numbers)

Horses	Cattle (all Dairy)	Sheep	Pigs	including Sows
22	24	150	315	25

Source: *Recensement Général de l'Agriculture*, 1956. Inventaire Communal.

Settlement and communications

Examination of map and photograph shows two types of settlement. Over most of the plain a dispersed pattern is the rule. The density of this varies; it is at its greatest to the south-east of Solliès Pont along the left bank of the Gapeau, and again north of Solliès Pont. This may well relate to the greater intensity of cultivation possible with irrigation. On the other hand, east of La Garde the number of farms seems to decrease—possibly due to the flooding hazard mentioned previously.

The second type of plain settlement is strongly nucleated. The growth of these settlements (Solliès Pont, La Farlède, La Crau, La Garde), is closely related to the physical geography and communications, and can be deduced easily from the map.

The future of farming in this area, as indeed over most of Mediterranean France, appears to be bound up with irrigation. The crops which produce the greatest return per hectare are vegetables and flowers. Thus we may well see an extension of this type of land use at the expense of the vine and tree crops. This is only possible with better water supplies, probably from the Durance basin to the north.

Exercises

1. Describe and account for the distribution of woodland in the area.
2. Explain the distribution of the various types of land use shown in fig. 20.
3. Why has Solliès Pont become the largest settlement in the area, while Solliès Ville has remained relatively small?
4. Explain the facts shown in the temperature and rainfall graphs for Cuers. How do these graphs depart from the characteristic 'Mediterranean' climate? Explain these differences.
5. What do you understand by the term 'river régime'? Discuss the importance of an understanding of river régimes in human geography, drawing your examples from contrasting rivers.
6. What additional information can be obtained about the Provençal landscape by using the photograph as well as the map?
7. Construct a rectangle 11 centimetres high and the same width as the map extract. Divide into 5 horizontal sections, the top one of 3 cm, the other four of 2 cm, height. In the top section draw an east–west section across the map through le Matheron (9905) and Solliès Ville (scale 1 cm to 200 metres). In the other four sections, draw accurate maps of *(a)* drainage features; *(b)* land use; *(c)* settlements; and *(d)* communications in the strip of land lying between northings 05 and 06. Comment on the geographical relationships revealed by your transects.

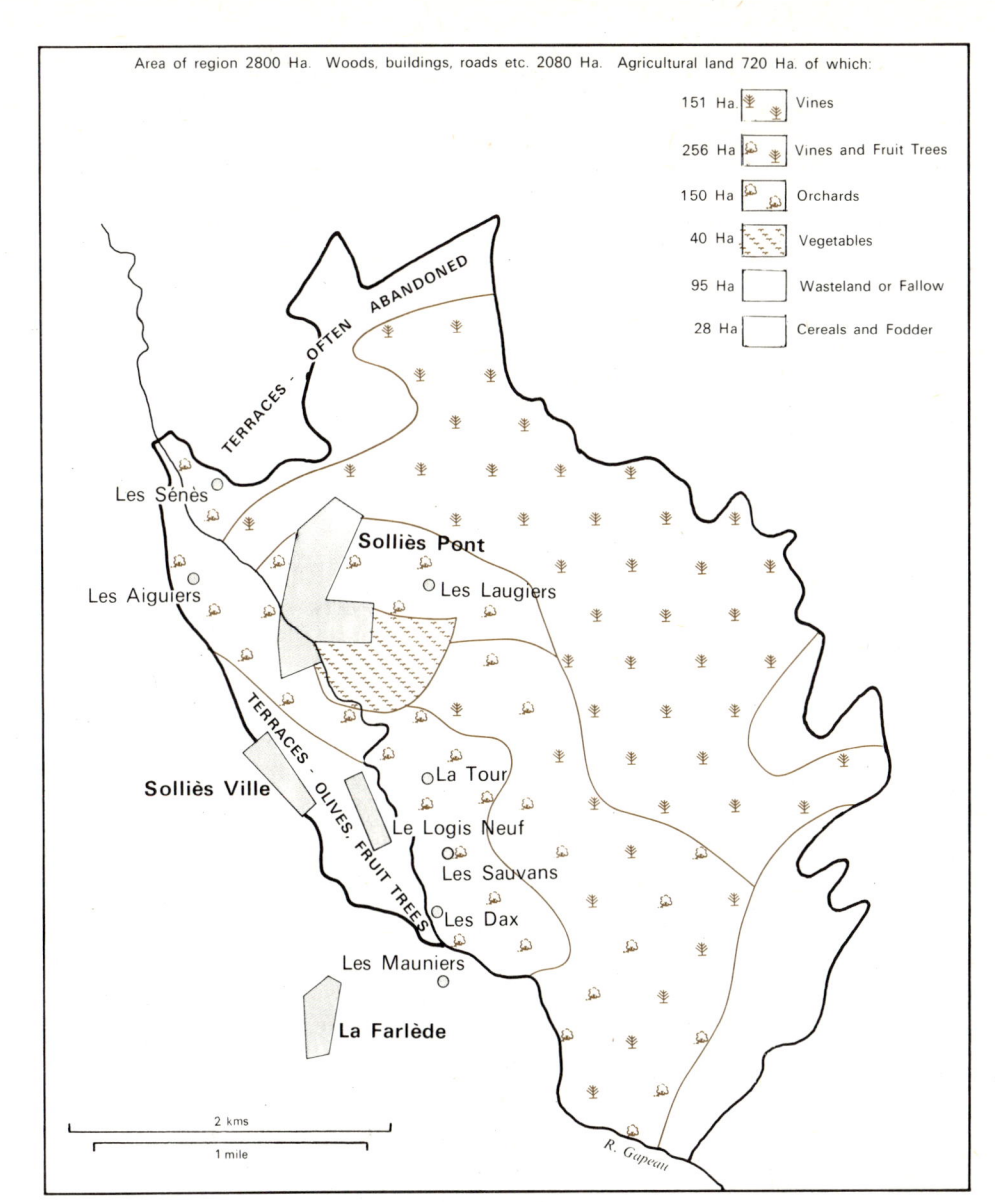

Figure 20. Land use around Solliès-Pont.

Further reading

EVANS, E. E. *France*, Christophers, 1954, chapters 4, 5 and 20.
LAMBERT, A. 'Farm consolidation in western Europe', Geography no 218, **47,** 1963.
MARTONNE, E. DE. *Geographical Regions of France*, 2nd edn, Heinemann 1941, chapter 14.
MONKHOUSE, F. J. *A Regional Geography of Western Europe*, Longmans 1965, chapter 15.
ORMSBY, H. *France*, Methuen, 1950, chapter 10.

**Study 15
MARSEILLES
BOUCHE-DU-
RHONE
FRANCE**

A Study of Port Growth.

Extract from Map Sheet
XXXI-45. Marseille.
French 1:50,000 Series.
(Type 1922)

Based on a survey of 1900-04.
Revised 1933-36.
Published 1941.
Partial revision 1966.
Vertical interval of contours
10 metres.

Reproduced from a map published
by Institut Géographique
National, Paris.

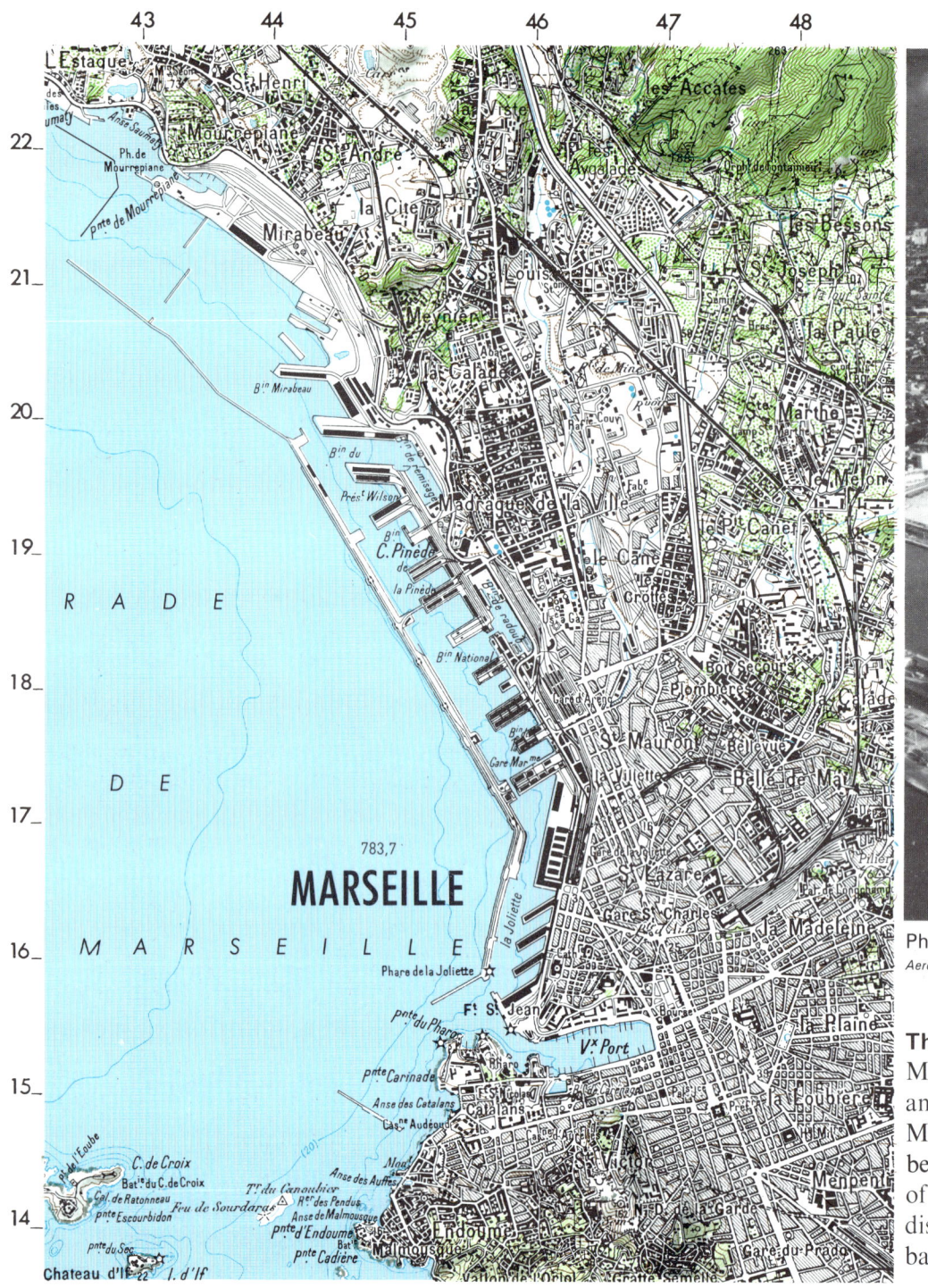

Map 16

Photograph 18. Marseilles. 19th century dock extensions.
Aerofilms Ltd., London.

The site and position of Marseilles

Marseilles, with a population of 936,000 in 1965, is the second largest city and first port of France and the most important and busiest port on the Mediterranean. One of the key factors enabling it to achieve this status has been its position near the southern end of the Rhône-Saône Corridor, one of the chief routeways in western Europe. However, the fact that the Rhône discharges into the Mediterranean by means of a delta with shifting sand banks and a shallow offshore gradient has precluded the development of a large seaport at the actual mouth of the river. To the west of the delta, longshore drifting has created a coast of sandbars and lagoons, so that the only place near the mouth of the river where a harbour might be created is to the east where a series of limestone hills, a continuation of the Pyreneean system, approaches the coast.

The site of the original settlement was around the shore of a small inlet on this deep water, virtually tideless and silt-free coast where some shelter is afforded by the surrounding hills and a group of small offshore islands, including the Ile Pomègues, Ile Rattoneau (just beyond the limits of the extract) and the Ile d'If. Around the original harbour, the present Vieux Port, is a belt of undulating ground beyond which a series of steep-sided hills rises up. To the north, east and south of Marseilles respectively lie the hills of the Chaîne de l'Estaque, Chaîne de l'Etoile and the Montagne Marseilleveyre (fig. 21). The city thus lies on a generally low plain surrounded by a semi-circle of hills and the Mediterranean. The site is in many ways an ideal one for a small settlement, but for a city of the size of Marseilles the steep bordering hills limit the space for the circulation of traffic and the expansion of industry and housing, so that very high building densities have resulted in the districts of the inner town. The surrounding hills are not evident from the map extract except in the north-east where the land rises to 263 metres in the district of les Accates and in the extreme south where a spot height of 162 metres is shown on the well-known sea mark of Notre Dame de la Garde (465142). A minor site element, but one which has played an important role in the development of the city, is the small limestone hill of St Laurent (unnamed on the extract) which lies to the immediate north of the Vieux Port (463158). It was on this hill, which protected the harbour at its foot from the *Mistral,* that the settlement had its beginnings.

The growth of Marseilles

The earliest settlement, Massilia, was founded about 600 B.C. by Greek merchants who recognised the advantages of the position of the small harbour, or Lacydon as it was named. Both the Greco-Roman and the medieval settlement occupied the same position on the St Laurent hill overlooking the port. The town subsequently expanded to the east and was enclosed by a wall at the end of the 14th century (fig 22). Until the end of the 17th century Marseilles remained within the limits of this wall, crowded with narrow streets and alleys running down the hill to the waterfront. Despite much recent demolition many of these narrow streets still remain to the south-east of the cathedral (460160). Following plans by Colbert for the development of the town, new walls were constructed between 1670 and 1690. These took in large areas to the east and south of the existing settlement and involved the construction of a number of wide boulevards and streets, often laid out in a rectilinear plan. This pattern of streets persists to the present time and is clearly seen on the extract to the immediate east and south-east of the Vieux Port. Demolition of the outer walls began in 1790, but even before that date it had proved impossible to restrain buildings within the fortifications and the town had already spread along the routes to Aix and Toulon.

However, Marseilles's greatest period of expansion came in the 19th century. The French settlement of Algeria which began in 1830 led to an expansion of trade between the two shores of the Mediterranean. The port traffic of Marseilles increased from 800,000 tons in 1827 to over 3 million tons in 1847, and increasingly in the 19th century Marseilles became the centre from which trade with North Africa was organised. In 1869 the

Figure 21. The position of Marseilles.

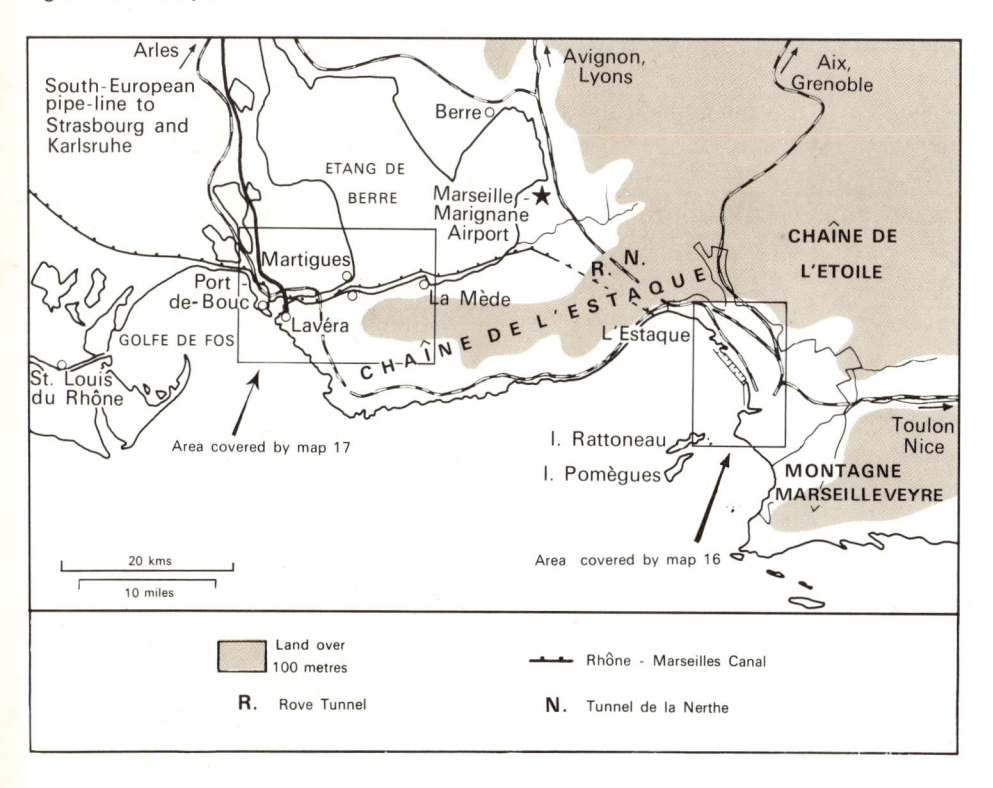

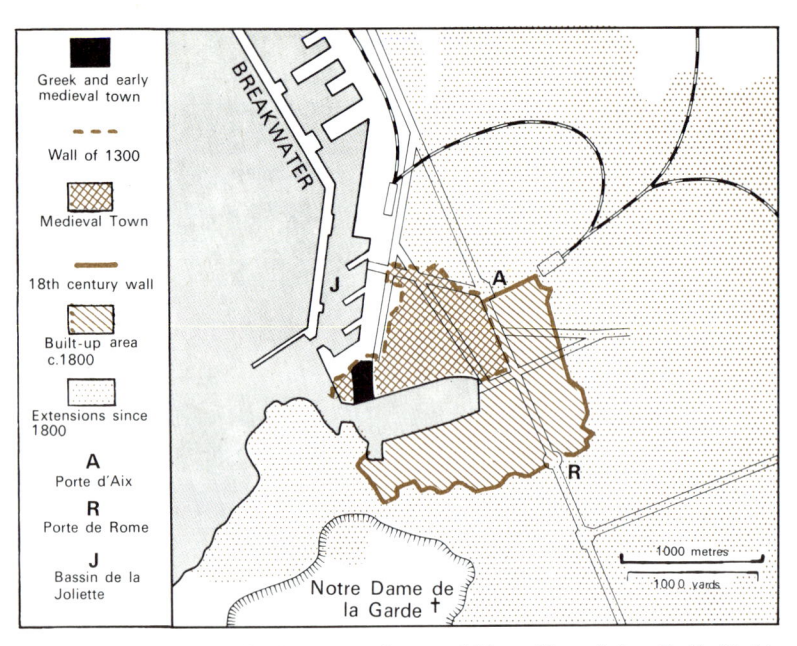

Figure 22. The growth elements of central Marseilles, (after R. E. Dickinson)

opening of the Suez Canal placed the town in a strong position for trade with the Far East and provided access to new sources of raw materials for the industrial development of the city. The trade of Marseilles has always been very closely connected with developments in Algeria. For example, Algerian independence led to a 60 per cent reduction in trade between Marseilles and North Africa, although another interesting result of this development was an influx of about 100,000 returning French to boost the population of the city from 784,000 in 1962 to 930,000 in 1964.

The 19th century growth of maritime trade necessitated extensions to the port. A small annexe to the Vieux Port was cut out of solid limestone on the south side of the natural harbour (460151), but this provided only a small addition to the existing docking space. The eventual solution took the form of major harbour works to the north of the Vieux Port. The shore of the Rade de Marseille was evened out and a great protective breakwater built some 500 metres out from the straightened shore in 10–15 metres of water. A series of projecting moles was constructed from the new shore to create a series of interconnected dock basins within the shelter of the breakwater. The first of these, the Bassin de la Joliette, was opened in 1853 and others followed to the north in rapid succession. At the same time the warehouses, silos, stations, sidings and harbour installations which are clearly seen on the map and photograph 18 were developed. Communications inland were also improved to deal with the increasing volume of trade. The Tunnel de la Nerthe was cut through the Chaîne de l'Estaque to carry a railway to Avignon and Lyons in 1852. This was followed by lines to Toulon and Grenoble in 1859 and 1877. In 1915 the Corniche line was constructed westwards along the rocky coast to Port-de-Bouc at the entrance to the Etang de Berre. In 1927 the four-mile-long Rove Tunnel through the Chaîne de l'Estaque was opened to carry the Marseilles-Rhône Canal northwards from l'Estaque to the Etang de Berre where it runs along the southern shore to Martigues. From there the navigation leads through the Etang de Caronte to Port-de-Bouc to connect with the Arles-Bouc Canal which runs northwestwards to join the Rhône (see fig 21 and map 17, showing the entrance to the Etang de Berre).

During the 19th and present centuries the city has expanded north and west on the low ground at the foot of the hills, although this naturally marshy ground, with its numerous streams such as the Ruisseau de Plombières and Ruisseau des Aygalades not named on the map, was far from an ideal site for urban development. As can be seen from the extract, the buildings and streets of the town are now climbing the heights of the Massif de la Garde and les Accates.

Many of the present day industries of Marseilles date back to the 19th century, especially those based on the processing of raw materials from Africa and the Far East. Within this group mention should be made of sugar-refining and the processing of fats and oils to produce soap, margarine and various edible oils. Other food industries include flour-milling and the manufacture of chocolate, jams, biscuits, semolina, etc. As in all large ports ship-repairing, marine-engineering and metal-working employ large numbers. Up to about 1920 the industry of Marseilles consisted almost entirely of these types, but in recent decades there has been a marked growth of a wide range of generally light industries, a trend which relates in part to the development of hydro-electric power resources in south-eastern France and partly to the government policy of decentralisation of industry, which makes a peripheral area such as Marseilles attractive for such developments. The chief industrial districts of the central town shown on the extract include St Lazare (4616), St Mauron (4617), Belle de Mai, Bellevue and Plombières (4717), and la Viste (4522).

From these remarks it is clear that the growth of Marseilles can be divided into two phases: a long initial period of development up to c. 1850 in which the growing town shows a submission to the conditions of its site, and secondly the modern growth after 1850, which has involved ambitious engineering projects (harbour works, tunnelling, land drainage, etc.) to overcome, in part at least, the natural limitations of the site and to enable the potential strength of the town's position to be realised.

The port of Marseilles

As mentioned above, the modern port of Marseilles lies within the shelter of the breakwater which has been progressively extended until it now exceeds 7 km in length. On the inner side of the breakwater a number of moles have been built out from the straightened shore to create a series of interconnected dock basins and a total length of over 30 km of quays. The virtually tideless nature of the Mediterranean means that ships can enter and leave at all times and no locks are needed at the dock entrances. The various quays are all connected by railway tracks to an elaborate system of sidings and the principal station serving the port, the Gare d'Arenc. The Gare de la Joliette serves the southern part of the harbour. The form of the harbour is well illustrated on photograph 18, which shows the Bassin du Président Wilson and Bassin de la Pinède in the foreground. Beyond the bascule bridge which links the breakwater with the shore can be seen the Bassin Nationale. The intensive use of the various jetties and the shore bordering the harbour is evident from the photograph. A striking cluster of silos, storage tanks and other buildings can be seen on the slightly higher ground of the former Cap Pinède. It is interesting to note that the Bassin de remisage, a former ship repairing basin, which is shown on the map extract, has been infilled and is in the process of being built upon. During

Details of the docks of Marseilles

Name of docks	Date of opening	Depth in metres	Cargoes handled	Chief trading connections	Other remarks
1. Le Bassin de la Joliette	1853	8-9	Fruit and *Primeurs*	Algeria, Tunisia, Morocco, Corsica, Israel, Senegal.	Largest of the dock basins. Quayside installations include fruit and vegetable markets, grain silos, wine stores and the harbour operations office. Gare de la Joliette deals almost exclusively with the fruit and vegetable trade.
2. Le Bassin de la Gare Maritime	1859	9	Ground nuts, copra, palm kernels, coal, sulphur, china clay.	Algeria, W. Africa, Greece, Turkey.	Takes name from maritime station formerly on one of the moles. Shown on map extract but now disused. Storage premises for bananas.
3. Le Bassin Nationale	1863	9	Varied cargoes—vegetable oils, grain, coal, etc.	Middle East, Greece, Turkey.	Vegetable oil storage installations on the quayside.
4. Le Bassin de Radoub	1863	9	None.	None.	This section of the harbour consists of 7 dry docks for ship repairing. (60% of all French ship repairing work is done in Marseilles.)
5. Le Bassin de la Pinède	1900	9.5	Varied cargoes—oil, tropical produce, grain, etc.	Malagasie, Réunion, Spain, Argentina, Italy.	Separated from the Bassin Nationale by a bascule bridge which carries a railway to the outer breakwater. (Not shown on the map). Grain silos, oil storage tanks.
6. Le Bassin du Président Wilson	1909	9-12	Imports of sugar, etc. Much passenger traffic.	Far East, S. America, Australia, W. Indies.	New storage premises under construction for storage of sugar and bauxite.
Le Bassin de remisage	A former ship repairing basin, now infilled. (see Photograph 18).				
7. Le Bassin Mirabeau	1940	9–18.3	Varied cargoes—much passenger traffic.	N. America, Central America, S. Africa, Australia, etc.	Greatest depths here. Largest liners operate from these northern docks. Floating docks for ship repairing.

Marseilles: port traffic 1965

Imports	Tons
Crude oil and petroleum products	44,003,806
Foodstuffs (fruit, vegetables, cereals, raw sugar, molasses, coffee, wine, etc.)	1,715,280
Metal ores and scrap metal	686,774
Vegetable oils	405,946
Fertilisers	258,664
Timber, cork	146,432
Chemicals	145,531
Iron and steel, and non-ferrous metals	114,530
Coal	99,601
Manufactured goods (machinery, textiles, paper, etc.)	84,937
Rubber	51,854
Other goods	314,261
Total Imports	**48,927,616**

of which total 44,485,893 tons (92·5%) was handled by the port annexes (almost entirely crude oil).

Exports	
Refined petroleum products	4,722,061
Manufactured goods (machinery, textiles, glass, etc.)	565,020
Foodstuffs (wine, sugar, flour, semolina)	468,497
Chemical products (plastics, soap, detergents)	389,598
Building materials (cement, bricks, tiles)	239,144
Iron and steel, and non-ferrous metals	132,188
Coal	61,643
Other goods	353,213
Total Exports	**6,931,364**

of which total 4,734,474 tons (68·7%) was handled by the port annexes.
(Source: *Trafic du Port de Marseille. Principaux Elements Statistiques* 1965. Chambre de Commerce et d'Industrie de Marseille, 1966.)

THE ENTRANCE TO THE ETANG DE BERRE
BOUCHES DU RHONE
FRANCE

A Zone of New Industrial and Harbour Developments.

Extracts from Map Sheets XXX-44 & 45 Istres, XXXI-44 Martigues and XXXI-45 Marseilles. French 1:50,000 Series.

Revisions.
Istres. Full Revision 1960
Martigues. Full Revision 1960 Partial Revision 1963
Marseilles. Partial Revision 1966.
Vertical interval of Contours 10 metres.

Reproduced from maps published by Institut Géographique National, Paris.

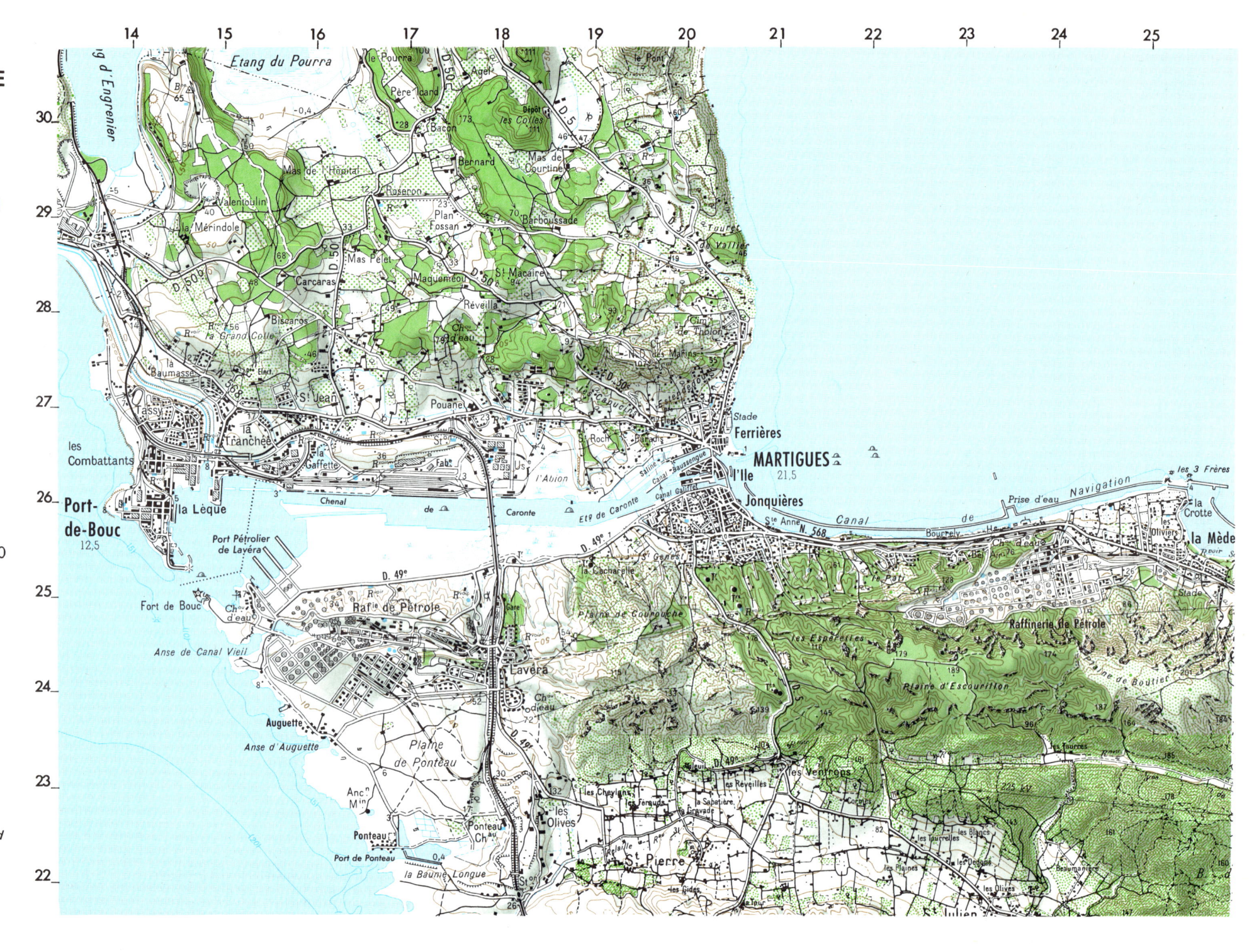

Map 17

Photograph 19. The Lavéra oil refinery, tanker terminal and petro-chemical plant.

British Petroleum Ltd., London.

83

the last 10 years many changes have taken place at the northern end of the harbour. The breakwater has been extended to the north-west to create a new dock basin. In the Mirabeau district an extensive area has recently been reclaimed from the sea and now includes quays, warehouses, dry docks, railway sidings etc. Building is continuing here at the present time. Details of the various dock basins are given in tabular form.

In 1965 Marseilles and its annexes ranked third among the ports of Europe (after Rotterdam and London) in terms of tonnage of goods loaded and unloaded, and handled 37% of French maritime trade. In that year the port handled almost 55 million metric tons of goods, dealt with 859,100 passengers and had over 21,000 arrivals and departures of vessels. Details of the export/import trade are shown on page 81.

A striking point about these figures is the fact that the port annexes of Marseilles (Port-de-Bouc, Lavéra, Martigues, La Mède and Berre) now handle more than eight times the tonnage of Marseilles itself. Part of this area of relatively new harbour installations and industry is shown on the second map extract of the Marseilles region.

The entrance to the Etang de Berre.
The exact location of the map area which lies 20 miles to the north-west of Marseilles is shown on fig 21. It should be noted that the extract is composed of sections of map from three different sheets of the 1:50,000 series, each with varying dates of revision. Thus, certain discrepancies occur along the north-south line 188 as, for example, the break in the road west of St. Pierre (188223).

Relief and drainage of the area bordering the entrance to the Etang de Berre
The southern part of the map extract shows the western end of the limestone hills of the Chaîne de l'Estaque. The pervious nature of the rocks in this area is indicated by the temporary and interrupted nature of most of the stream courses, the large number of dry valleys and the need for numerous reservoirs for the storage of water. The hills gradually decline in elevation westwards, but drop steeply northwards to the Etang de Berre and the Chenal de Caronte. This northern edge is dissected by a series of short dry valleys, as to the south of Martigues. The summits of the Plaine d'Escourillon and the Plaine de Boutier, where a maximum elevation of 201 metres is attained (253242), show a marked flattening. In the extreme south the large valley of St Pierre runs eastwards into the hills for over 5 km, but of greater interest is the unusual form and drainage pattern of the smaller *vallon* (abb. *von*) which lies high above the level of the main valley and runs east-west approximately along the level of grid line 23. The higher parts of the Chaîne de l'Estaque are heavily wooded apart from the Plaine de Boutier which, like the western slopes, has a cover of *garrigue* vegetation. To the north of the Chenal de Caronte is another area of hilly ground, although in this instance the relief is generally lower and more subdued, and rarely rises above 100 metres. In the north-west two depressions lie just below sea level and are occupied by the lagoons of Engrenier and Pourra. The margins of the latter are subject to wide seasonal fluctuations. In the area north of the Chenal de Caronte the woodland is more broken and interspersed with areas of vines and olives. The shores of the channel linking the Etang de Berre and the Mediterranean are flanked by low, marshy ground which reaches almost 1 km in width to the north-west of Lavéra.

The map extract provides little information about navigation channels in this area. The Mediterranean is shown to have a fairly gentle offshore profile, while the Etang de Berre is uniformly shallow at a depth of 5-10 metres. The map fails to reveal the fact that the Chenal de Caronte has had a channel over 10 metres deep dredged through it, while a similar channel has been made across the Etang de Berre continuing the line of the marker buoys east of Martigues. This enables tankers to reach the terminal at Berre on the north-eastern shore of the lagoon.

Settlement and industrial development
Away from the coast settlement is scattered. In the south the higher parts of the limestone hills are virtually devoid of settlement. The two largest settlements are Martigues and Port-de-Bouc at either end of the Chenal de Caronte. Martigues, which occupies land on either side of the channel together with the Ile Jonquières is shown to have a population of 21,500, but this has increased since the publication of the map to over 25,000. Similarly the population of Port-de-Bouc is now some 2,000 greater than the 12,500 indicated on the map. La Mède occupies a quite steeply sloping site at the mouth of a large valley which penetrates west into the hills. Lavéra is a vast complex of industrial developments, but the actual settlement to the east of the railway remains quite small.

The industrial and port developments of the Etang de Berre were due to the impossibility of extending the port of Marseilles beyond l'Estaque, and also the lack of extensive sites in the city for expanding industry, especially the petrochemical industry which, as can be seen from photograph 19, requires a vast area of ground. First developments around the lagoon began in the early 1920s; the first oil refinery was introduced in 1931 and this industry has shown a phenomenal growth since the war. Imports of crude oil to the refineries of the Etang de Berre totalled over 43 million tons in 1965 compared with 3 million tons in 1948. Three refineries now operate around the shores of the lagoon, at Lavéra (Sté Française des Petroles B.P.), La Mède (Cie Française de Raffinage) and Berre (Sté Shell-Berre). In addition to these, a new refinery (Esso) was opened in 1965 at Fos-sur-Mer some 2 km to the north-west of the map extract. This latter development is in fact the beginning of an enormous project planned to create a completely new tanker terminal and industrial zone on the shore of the Golfe de Fos. At the present time deep approach channels are being dredged and new dock basins and breakwaters constructed, so that when completed in 1968 the terminal will be used by 100,000-ton tankers. The Lavéra terminal, constructed in 1952, can accommodate tankers of up to 70,000 tons. In 1962 a pipe-line (Le Pipe-Line Sud-Européan) was opened between Lavéra and Strasbourg and Karlsruhe, thus shortening the route for oil to that area by 1,500 km compared with the route via the North Sea and Rotterdam.

In 1965 the four refineries imported 43 million tons of crude oil from the Saharan and Middle East oilfields, 27.5 million tons of which was piped directly to the Rhine valley and 15.6 million tons refined locally.

Sources of crude oil 1965

Libya	50%
Saudi Arabia	25%
Algeria	14%
Syria and Lebanon[1]	9%
Iran	7%
Tunisia	7%

Output of refineries 1965

La Mède	5.8 M. tons
Berre	5.2 M. tons
Lavéra	4.2 M. tons
Fos-s-Mer[2]	0.4 M. tons
	15.6 M. tons
	(27% of French refined production)

[1]From pipe-line terminals at Baniyas, Tripoli and Sidon for oil from Iraq and Saudi Arabia.
[2]Operations started July 1965.
Source: *Port de Marseille 1965*. Direction du Port Autonome de Marseille 1966.

The industrial developments of the district are basically concerned with oil refining, but an impressive range of ancillary petrochemical industries has also developed. These include the manufacture of carbon black for the paint and rubber industries, ethylene, propylene and other plastics, captane, acetones, detergents, insecticides etc. These industries are found on the north bank of the Chenal de Caronte and also in close proximity to the refineries of Lavéra and La Mède. On photograph 19 the oil refinery is shown in the centre of the view, while the extensive plant in the lower left of the photograph consists of the associated chemical industry. These complex industrial developments represent the present stage reached in a long and continuous evolution of harbour works and industries in the Marseilles region, an evolution which has its beginnings in the Greek trading post established on the St Laurent Hill more than 2,500 years ago. The future of Marseilles lies in the establishment of efficient communications with its hinterland. Already the South European Pipe-Line enables it to serve the Rhine Rift Valley. The development of a complete waterway link with the Rhine would strengthen this connection and enable Marseilles to compete with Rotterdam and Europort in serving this interior part of Europe.

Exercises

1. Amplify the statement that Marseilles occupies a poor site but an excellent position for a modern seaport.
2. Examine the effects of the following on the development of Marseilles:
(a) the opening of the Suez Canal; *(b)* the history of French settlement in Algeria; *(c)* the opening of trans-Alpine railway routes.
3. It has been pointed out that Marseilles has a similar site, position and history of development as Genoa. Examine the truth of this statement.
4. Compare the new industrial and harbour developments in the Marseilles region with the Europort developments of Rotterdam.
5. What criteria may be used to classify ports?
6. Examine the conditions necessary for the establishment of large scale oil refining and petrochemical industries.
7. With reference to the map of the Etang de Berre, draw an annotated contour sketch map of the area in the south west bounded by easting 21 and northing 25. In what ways is the drainage pattern of this area unusual? Suggest how it may have evolved.

Further reading

BOYLE, P. S. 'Le Nouveau Port Petrolier de Lavéra: Expansion Portuaire de Marseille.' *Review de Géographie Alpine*. Vol. 48. no 3. 1960.
DICKINSON, R. E. *The West European City*, 2nd edn, Routledge and Kegan Paul 1961, chapter 18.
France, vol. IV, Naval Intelligence Geographical Handbook Series, 1942.
HOYLE, B. S. Recent Port Expansion and Associated Industrial Development at Marseilles, *Tijdschrift Voor Economische en Sociale Geografie*. no 3. March 1960.
JONES, H. D. 'Marseilles Looks Ahead', *Geographical Magazine* XXV, May 1952.
MARTONNE, E. DE. *Geographical Regions of France*, 2nd edn, Heinemann, 1941, chapter 14.
MONKHOUSE, F. J. *A Regional Geography of Western Europe*, Longmans, 1965, chapter 15.
MORGAN, F. W. and BIRD, J. *Ports and Harbours*, 2nd edn, Hutchinson, 1958.
ORMSBY, H. *France*, 2nd edn, Methuen 1950, chapter 10.
PIERREIN, L. 'Les Constants de l'Evolution Economique et les Problèmes d'Avenir', *La Revue de la Chambre de Commerce de Marseille*, **756**, 1965.
PIERREIN, L. 'Sur l'Expansion Economique de Marseille et sa Région', *Bulletin de Géographie d'Aix-Marseille*, **66**, 1955.
SIEGFRIED, A. *The Mediterranean*, Cape, 1948.
TOMKINSON, D. 'The Marseilles Experiment', *Town Planning Review*, **24**, 1953.

Pamphlets issued by the Petroleum Information Bureau.
The Port of Lavéra. October 1963.
From Mediterranean to Rhine. December 1963.

Study 16
THE ENGADINE GRISONS SWITZERLAND

An Alpine Valley.

Extract from Map Sheet 249. Tarasp. Swiss 1:50,000 Series.

Map Published 1951.
Revised 1964.
Vertical interval of contours 20 metres.

Extract from the Swiss National Map 1:50,000 reproduced with the permission of the Topographical Survey of Switzerland of 5 December, 1967.

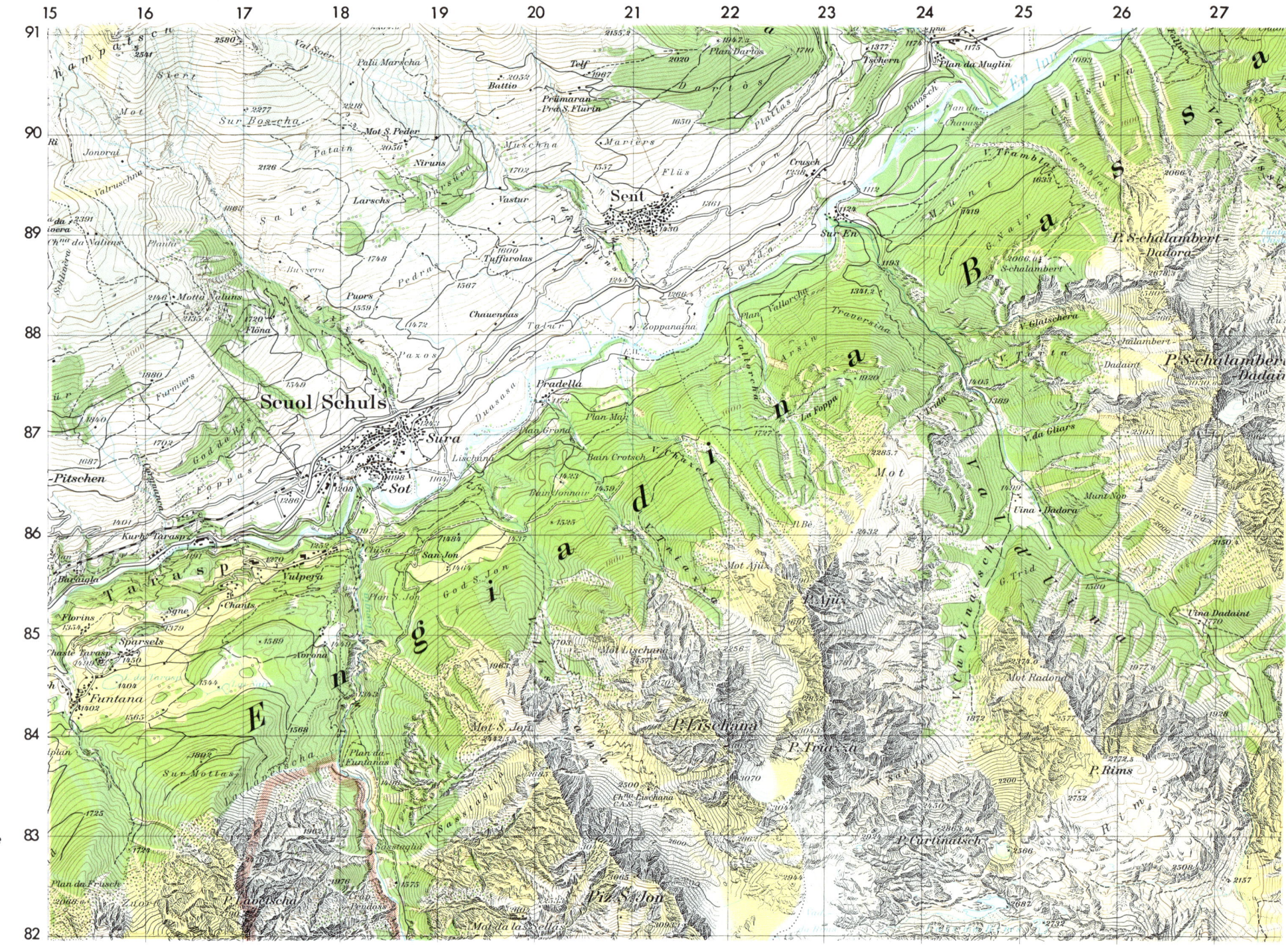

Map 18

Photograph 20. Part of the Engadine valley. Notice the cultivated terraces, the forested north-facing slopes and the incised river.

Swiss National Tourist Office, London.

The map extracts of the Gorner Glacier and the Lower Engadine are taken from the Swiss 1:50,000 series. These maps, like their companion series at 1:25,000 and 1:100,000 are distinguished by very fine draughtsmanship and in particular by the excellent manner in which relief is shown. Contours are normally drawn at a 20 metre vertical interval, but on parts of the Gorner Glacier a 10 metre interval is used to give a clearer impression of relief. On steep rocky slopes a fine rock drawing technique is employed, and over the whole map a system of oblique hill shading emphasises the general pattern of relief. The combination of these three methods gives a clear impression of landscapes which are complicated and which have a considerable range of altitude within short distances.

The map extract shows a section of the Engadine region which is located in the eastern part of Switzerland and is drained by the River Inn in an easterly direction towards Austria. A comparison of the map and photograph will illustrate many of the essential geographical features common to a large number of Alpine valleys.

Relief
The southern peaks show many characteristics of recent glacial and frost action. In fact, small ice-patches, hardly large enough to be designated glaciers, still occupy the higher parts (c. 2,800 metres) of the Val da Lischana (2282) and Val Triazza (2283). The heads of these valleys are rounded in plan with steep back and side walls and are separated from each other and from the adjacent Val Curtinatsch by steep-sided ridges or arêtes.

Further down, both valleys show evidence of recent ice extension to lower levels. Melt-water from the small corrie glaciers loses itself in piles or morainic material only to issue $1\frac{1}{2}$ to 2 km away and some 900 metres lower down the valleys.

The peaks are represented on the map by a combination of contours, rock shading and oblique hill shading. These convey an impression of ruggedness and steepness which is borne out when reference is made to the photograph. For much of the year crevices and hollows contain snow and ice, and alternate freezing and melting in response to wide diurnal ranges of temperature is responsible for the weathering of the bare slopes, thus producing a rough and angular surface with scree lower down. Deep gullies are cut in the lower slopes by melt-water armed with angular debris.

Evidence that ice once extended to much lower levels is afforded by the appearance of both main and tributary valleys. Both the Clemgia and Val d'Uina streams show a longitudinal profile which hangs into the main valley. The upper parts of each of these valleys have gentle gradients, and in the case of the Val d'Uina a width sufficient for habitation and possibly cultivation (2486 and 2685). Lower down, each valley narrows and reaches the floor of the Inn trench through steep-sided gorges of considerable gradient, which were cut in post-glacial times by river action. (Note especially the stream in squares 1884 and 1885.)

The Inn valley has a flat floor which contrasts strongly with the steepness of its sides. This fact, together with the absence of spurs extending into the valley, supports the theory that a large valley glacier once occupied the Inn trench. At higher levels, discontinuous benches are observable along the valley which probably represent the remains of the pre-glacial valley sides before over-deepening took place. Parts of these benches are visible in the photograph, notably in the centre where a small clearing (San Jon 1,464 metres) is to be seen. Similarly on the northern side in the village of Sent a bench can be noted at 1,430 metres. Since glacial times a considerable amount of erosion has been accomplished. The river now flows some 80 metres below the level of the low terrace (1786), although further downstream the entrenchment of the river is much less. Some widening at the present river level has taken place, notably by Scuol-Sot (1886), Duasasa (1987) and in square 2389.

Land use
The most remarkable feature of the land use on both the map and photograph is the contrast between the two sides of the Inn trench. On the southern side of the valley the greater part of the land is forested with larch and fir up to the treeline at about 2,000 metres. On the northern side forests are far less common, being limited to the steep sides of the tributary valley north of Scuol and a few patches on the slopes north of Sent. Instead, most of this northern side is covered by pasture land, though not always of the highest quality. Marshy ground is shown at intervals and loose rock is occasionally in evidence. The low terrace of the Inn valley is shown in the photograph to be intensively cultivated on the northern side. A variety of cropping is carried out to the very edge of the terrace and for a short distance up the slopes of the north side. On the south side of the valley there seems to be little evidence of farming. A few clearings with buildings occur in the woodland, and also further up the tributary valleys as at Uina Dadora (2486), but these are probably for hay and grazing rather than cropping. (Note the San Jon clearing on the photograph.) On the upper slopes north of the Inn there are far more of these isolated buildings; twenty-nine north of the Inn valley above 1,500 metres compared with eleven south of the valley. It seems probable that these pasturelands are for use during the summer

only and correspond to the mayens of Central Switzerland. In comparison, the height of the mayen in the Val d'Anniviers in Valais is at 1,970 metres, and the highest pasture or alp occurs between 2,200 and 2,800 metres.

The contrast in land use between the north-facing and south-facing slopes can be directly attributed to differences in insolation rather than to differences of slope. The proximity of peaks such as Piz Ajûz, Piz Lisehana and Piz S. Jon considerably reduces the hours of sunlight on the north-facing slopes during much of the year. This is particularly important during the spring and autumn seasons, when the sun is at a moderate angle of elevation and when crops and pasture are at the beginning or climax of their growth cycle. For a full discussion of these problems and for an explanation of the methods of calculating the duration and intensity of insolation, reference should be made to the work on alpine valleys by A. Garnett.

Settlement and communications

Both major settlements, Scuol and Sent, owe their position to the availability of land for cropping and pasture. Their actual siting on the northern side of the valley is dictated by the suitability of slopes for building. An examination of the map will show that Scuol has two nuclei: Scuol-Sura is built on gently sloping land at a point where the stream issuing from the valley of La Clozza has built up an alluvial fan, while Scuol-Sot is on a terrace close to the entrenched River Inn. Both settlements were originally agricultural centres, but tourism has stimulated their growth in recent decades, particularly along the roads leading out of the town. Sent is considerably higher than Scuol (1,430 metres compared with 1,200 metres at Scuol) and is sited on a fairly level bench some 300 metres above the floor of the valley. The factor of insolation to which reference has already been made probably has an influence here. Tarasp-Vulpera owes its development mainly to its reputation as a health resort based on mineral waters, the Kurhaus being a hotel in which a mineral water treatment may be taken.

Lines of communication inevitably follow the river valley. Scuol is the terminus of a single track railway which runs north-east from St Moritz and links with Italian and Swiss railways through the Bernina and Albula Passes. The growth of Scuol and Tarasp as tourist resorts is connected with this development. Roads follow the sides of the valley at two distinct levels on the northern side and link the larger settlements. It is noteworthy that there is no continuous road connection on the southern side of the valley, and the section of road that does exist merely serves the tourist centres of Tarasp and Vulpera. The hills are served only by tracks which frequently take tortuous hairpin courses to link the higher pasturelands with the valley.

Until the late 19th century the Engadine was one of the most isolated parts of the Alps. Communications up the Inn valley to the rest of Switzerland and to Italy entailed difficult crossings of the Maloja, Bernina or Julier Passes, while downstream the route to Austria was made hazardous by the Finstermunz Gorge. This area has preserved its own language of Romansch, although some of the more important features also have German names, for example, Romansch—Scuol, German—Schuls. The following Romansch terms frequently occur on the map extract, and a knowledge of their meaning aids interpretation:

Plan Terrace, plateau
Piz Peak
Mot A summit of the ridge culminating in the peak of that name.
Vadret abb. Vad. Glacier
Lai Lake

The combination of valley cultivation, upland pasture, forestry and tourism is today characteristic of many Alpine valleys, not only in Switzerland but also in Austria and France. Interesting comparisons can be made with the Rhône valley near Sion and with many Austrian examples. Seldom though is the distinction so clear between sunny, cultivated, south-facing slopes (*adret* or *sonnenseite*) and the shaded, forested, north-facing slopes (*ubac* or *schattenseite*).

Exercises

1. The large settlement on the lefthand side of the photograph is Scuol. Give a map reference for the point from which the photograph was taken. What is the direction and angle of view of the photograph?
2. Construct a longitudinal profile of the stream in Val d'Uina from the spot height 2157 metres (2782) to its confluence with the River Inn. Try to explain any peculiarities of its course.
3. Plot on a sheet of tracing paper the settlements on the map extract. Comment on their distribution in relation to *(a)* relief; *(b)* land use; *(c)* communications.
4. Note the height of each settlement on the map above 1500 metres. Construct a frequency curve for settlement distribution by plotting on graph paper the number of settlements at different heights. What conclusions can you draw from your graph?
5. With reference to a wide range of examples, discuss the influence of slopes on agriculture and settlement.

Further reading

EVANS, E. E. 'Transhumance in Europe', *Geography*, **25**, no 4, 1940.
GARNETT, A. 'Insolation, topography and settlement in the Alps', *Geographical Review*, **25**, 1935, p. 601.
GARNETT, A. 'Insolation and Relief', *Trans. of the Institute of British Geographers*, **5**, 1937.
MUTTON, A. F. A. *Central Europe*, Longmans, 1968, chapters 5 and 6.
PEATTIE, R. 'Limits of mountain economies', *Geographical Review* **21**, 1931.
PEATTIE, R. *Mountain Geography*, Harvard U.P., 1936.

Study 17
THE GORNER GLACIER VALAIS SWITZERLAND

Extract from Map Sheet 284. Mischabel. Swiss 1:50,000 Series.

Map published 1941. Revised 1965. Vertical interval of contours 20 metres. (Form lines with 10 metre vertical interval are marked on parts of the glacier.)

Extract from the Swiss National Map 1:50,000 reproduced with the permission of the Topographical Survey of Switzerland of 5 December, 1967.

Photograph 21. Tributaries of the Gorner Glacier and corries on the flank of the Breithorn.

Swiss National Tourist Office, London.

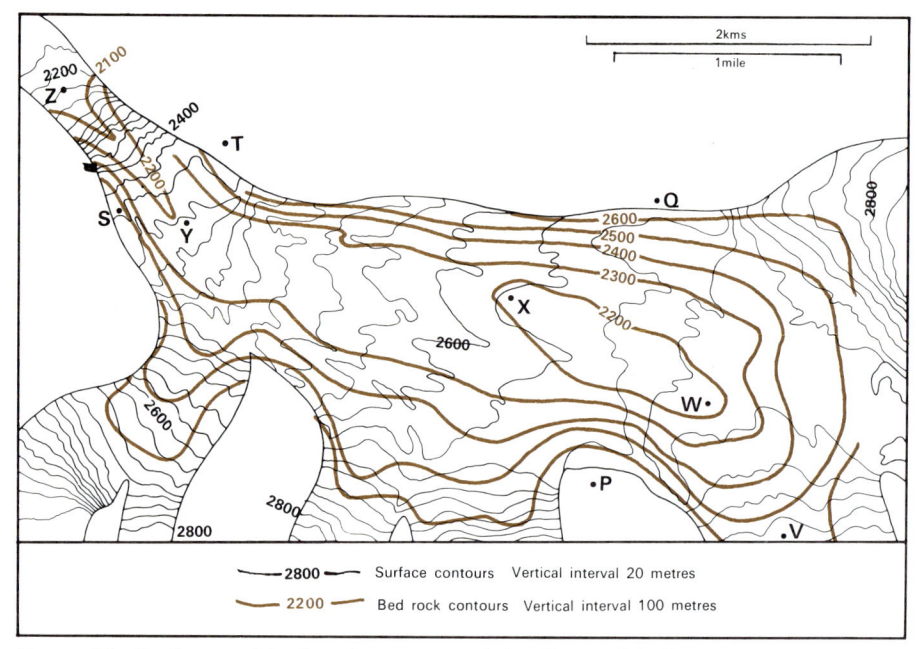

Figure 23. Surface and bed rock contours of the Gorner Glacier.
Based on Geologischer Atlas der Schweiz, 1:25,000, Blatt 535.

Certain of the highland regions of North-West Europe still contain active glaciers. The region shown on the map extract is part of the Pennine Alps of southern Switzerland. To the north, the Gorner Glacier drains to the valley of the Mattervispa which is tributary to the Rhône, while to the south of the watershed lies the Valle d'Aosta drained by the Dora Baltea, which is tributary to the River Po. The highlands of the area culminate in the Monte Rosa massif (4634 metres) in the south-eastern corner of the map. These are formed mainly of crystalline and metamorphic rocks. (A useful general account of the structure of the Alps can be found in A. F. A. Mutton's *Central Europe* or M. R. Shackleton's *Europe*.) Comparison of maps and photographs will suggest certain features of glacier movement, erosion and deposition. Perhaps the most characteristic feature of mountain glaciation is the corrie. Photograph 21 shows details of the corrie at the head of the Breithorn Glacier. The precipitous back and side walls are covered at their lower levels with the steep-surfaced corrie glacier (gradient of 1 in 1, or 45°). After a more gentle slope in the base of the corrie the glacier steepens once again in an impressive ice fall where a maze of crevasses runs transversely across the ice. Crevassing is shown on the map by discontinuous blue lines, and careful examination of the map shows a tendency for these to occur wherever the slope of the glacier steepens. Because of great pressure, ice may flow in a pseudo-plastic manner in its lowest layers, but, in its upper layers, it behaves as a crystalline mass, and irregularities of the valley floor which cause a steepening of its surface may encourage cracks which lie transversely to its course. Crevasses may also be found at the margins of glaciers as a result of tensions produced by the differing rates of movement of the centre and sides of the glacier. Because of the higher velocity towards the centre, tensions are produced which crack the ice along lines at 45° up-glacier, though these are soon rotated and deformed by differential flow. Longitudinal crevasses are often formed where the valley widens. Reference to squares 2392, 2489, 2589, 2888 and 3189 will illustrate the various types mentioned. In places the glacier surface has a number of convexities which relate to confluent tributaries. Unlike rivers, the contributions of tributaries do not mix with the main stream. The main ice mass is the Grenzgletscher, and this ice reaches the snout. That of the tributary on the northern side of Ob dem See (2990) does not reach the snout but only as far as the Rifelh^n. (2492.)

The map and photographs show abundant evidence of melt-water flow during the summer. By far the greater part finds its way beneath the surface ice (note the disappearance of surface streams down moulins to issue beyond the rocky terminal moraine as a wide and rushing torrent near Zermatt, which lies 3 km to the north of the map). At 2890 and 2990 and on photograph 22, lakes are to be found where the Monte Rosagletscher joins the main ice stream. Examination of the contours will show that the surface of the Grenzgletscher is over 20 metres above the surface of the lakes and in fact blocks the path of melt-water from Monte Rosagletscher, so forming these two lakes. Numerous surface depressions may be noted on the surface of the lower section of the glacier. Many of these relate to hollows formed and abandoned by meandering melt-water streams which have found outlets below the ice further upstream. In the summer these hollows are occupied by melt-water which, warmed by insolation, tends to enlarge them.

On photograph 21, below the ice fall of the Breithorn Gletscher, a marked light and dark arc-shaped banding is evident. These bands are *ogives* and their origin is a matter of some controversy. The foot of an ice fall is a zone of intense compression while the ice fall itself is an area of tension. It is thought that ice passing over the fall in summer is partially melted and recrystallisation with compression at the foot of the ice fall produces a dark band. In winter however there is no melting and compression produces a different form of ice which shows up as a white arc.

The frost-shattered slopes above the ice are the source of debris which accumulates as lateral moraine along the sides of glaciers. The convergence of two such lateral moraines produces a medial moraine as on the north side of Schmärze (spot height 2632 metres in 2690). Towards the snout of the glacier (2392, 2292 and 2293) the ice is almost completely covered with rocky debris, so that it is difficult to tell where the glacier ends and the terminal moraine begins.

The map gives no indication of the retreat of this glacier. Figures provided by measurement over a period of years show that the lower part of the glacier is wasting away rapidly. Near the snout a lowering of the surface at a rate of over 3 metres per year has occurred since 1930. Further upstream the rate declines until between Ob dem See and Schmärze the loss has been about 1·4 metres. This wastage affects the position of the snout, which is now at least $\frac{1}{2}$ km to the south-east of the position shown on the map.

Exercises

1. Find the widths, in yards, of the various glaciers shown on photograph 22. What is the distance in miles from the small peak in the left foreground to the peak (Dufourspitze) in the background?
2. Determine the point from which photograph 21 was taken.
3. Draw a longitudinal profile down the centre of the Grenzgletscher and Gornergletscher between the following spot heights: 4436 (Parrot Sp.—3385), 3923, 3113, 2664, and 1939. (Use mm/cm graph paper and a vertical scale of 1 cm:200 metres).
(a) Comment on the profile so obtained; *(b)* Calculate the vertical exaggeration of your section; *(c)* Calculate the actual surface gradients of
(i) The steepest section of the glacier. (ii) The least steep part of the glacier.
4. With reference to fig 23, construct the following three sections: *(a)* Down the centre of the Grenzgletscher to the 2200 metre contour through points V, W, X, Y, Z; *(b)* across the glacier between points P and Q; *(c)* across the glacier between points S and T.
On each section show (i) the surface of the glacier (ii) the bedrock. Comment on and try to account for the features revealed by your sections.
5. On a sheet of tracing paper mark *(a)* the landscape which is not covered with ice; *(b)* the pattern of moraines. Attempt to classify these moraines. Comment on the sources of material and position of these features.
6. Compare and contrast the corries on the eastern and western sides of the ridge from Signalkuppe (3486) to spot height 3636 (3491).
7. 'The modification of mountain landscapes by ice action can take many and varied forms.' Discuss.
8. Why do glaciers retreat?

Further reading

HOLMES, A. E. *Principles of Physical Geology,* Nelson, 1965, chapter 20.
MUTTON, A. F. A. *Central Europe,* Longmans, 1968, chapter 4.
SHACKLETON, M. R. *Europe,* Longmans, 1965, chapter 23.
SHARP, R. P. 'Glaciers', *Condon Lectures, Eugene, Oregon* 1960. University of Oregon Press.
SPARKS, B. W. *Geomorphology,* Longmans, 1960, chapter 12.

Photograph 22. The Gorner Glacier and Monte Rosa.
Swissair - Photo AG Zurich.

Key Symbols

Only those symbols necessary for interpretation of the map extracts have been listed. These are not comprehensive lists of symbols.

- ⊢⊢⊢⊢⊢ 'Länder' boundary
- 'Regierungsbezirk' boundary
- 'Kreis' boundary
- *Bahnhof* Railway, standard gauge multi-track with station
- *Haltepunkt* Railway, standard gauge single track with halt
- Narrow gauge railway
- Rack railway
- Tramway or industrial railway
- *im Bau* Autobahn — under construction
- 10 Main road
- L 1.0 A class with bordering trees
- L 1.0 A class with kilometre stone
- All weather road, light surface
- Fair weather road, loose surface
- Track
- Footpath with stiles
- Church with two spires
- Church with one spire
- Chapel
- Shrine
- Cemetery
- Monument
- Tower
- Chimney
- Tower or Chimney on a building
- Ruins
- Water-mill
- Forester's house
- Mine, in use
- Mine, disused
- Cave
- Sports ground

West German 1 : 50 000 Map Series

- Camping place
- -149 Spot height
- △307 Trigonometrical point
- Trig. point on church, tower, chimney
- Iron bridge
- Wooden bridge
- W.F. Ferry, railway, vehicle, pedestrian
- Steep edge (usually artificial)
- Embankment, with track
- Embankment, without track
- Stone quarry, pit
- Tumulus
- Wall, fence
- Hedge
- Low bank with hedge
- High tension cable
- Deciduous forest
- *Schneise* Coniferous forest
- Tree nursery
- Mixed forest
- Trees and shrubs
- Regularly spaced trees
- Orchard, with or without meadow
- Heath with scattered trees and shrubs
- Pasture with marsh, trees and bushes
- Vineyard
- Hop garden
- Garden
- Park

ABBREVIATIONS

A.T.	Observation tower	N.S.G.	Nature reserve
Bf.	Railway station	P.Wk.	Pumping station
Br.	Well	R.	Ruin
El.Wk.	Power station	Sch.	Barn
Fbr.	Factory	Schl.	Castle
H.Hs.	Hut, house	St.	Stable
Hbf.	Main railway station	S.Wk.	Sawmill
Hp.	Halt	T.	Tower
Jg.Hb.	Youth hostel	U.Wk.	Transformer station
K.D.	Monument of cultural interest	W.T.	Water tank
K.O.	Lime works	W.F.	Car ferry
Kp.	Chapel	Whs.	Inn
Krkhs.	Hospital	Wbh.	Water tower
M.	Mill	Zgl.	Brick yard
N.D.	Outstanding natural feature eg. large rock		

Dry river bed, Sluice, kilometre mark, Hollow, Spring, Limit of navigation, Weir, Lock, Plateau, Well, Drainage ditches, River, Ford, Hill top, Rocks, Old water course, Waterfall, Dry Ditch, Water tank, Marsh, Variable shore line, Groyne, Direction of flow, temporary lake or stream, Embankment (Wall), Reeds, Sand, Subterranean stream, Mole, Landing Stage, Valley, Peat digging, Height of water, Lake, Bathing place, Island

Contours:
- 100 metres
- 10 metres
- 5 metres
- 2.5 metres

French 1 : 50 000 Map Series

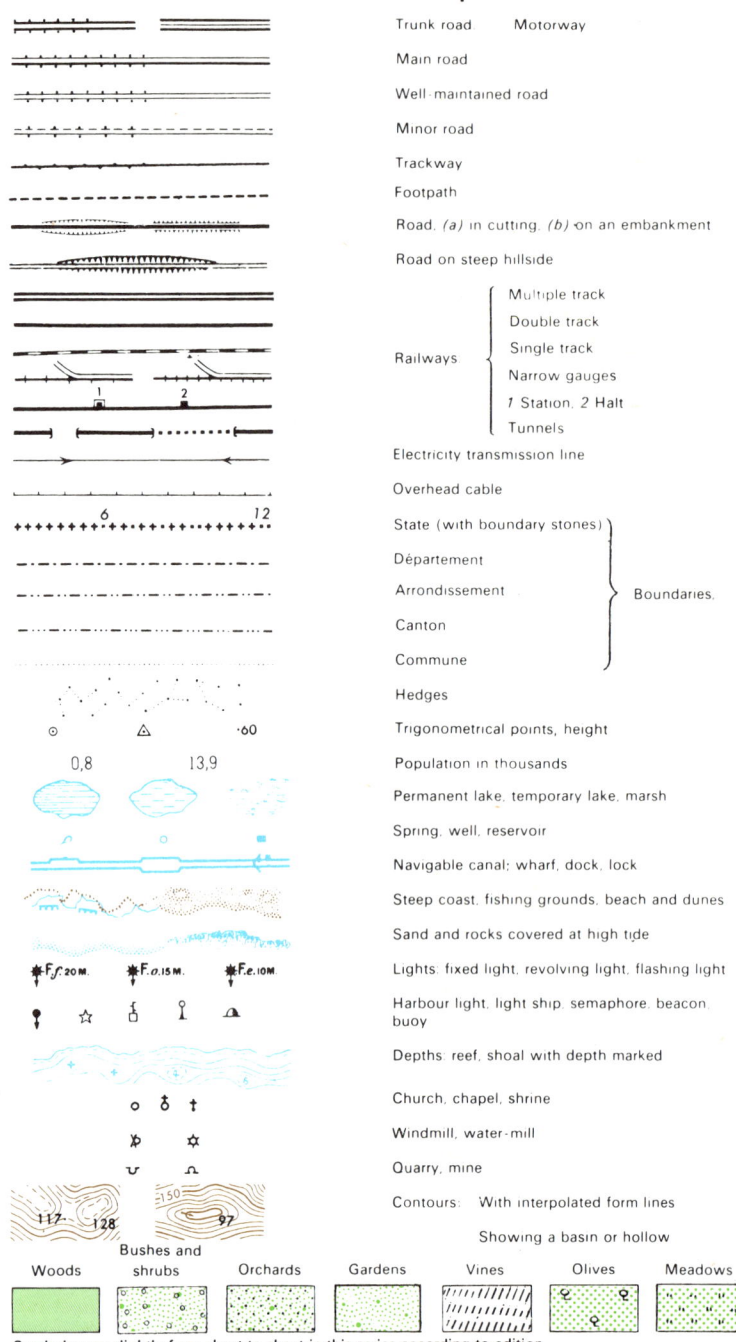

- Trunk road, Motorway
- Main road
- Well-maintained road
- Minor road
- Trackway
- Footpath
- Road, (a) in cutting, (b) on an embankment
- Road on steep hillside
- Railways { Multiple track, Double track, Single track, Narrow gauges, 1 Station, 2 Halt, Tunnels }
- Electricity transmission line
- Overhead cable
- Boundaries: State (with boundary stones), Département, Arrondissement, Canton, Commune
- Hedges
- Trigonometrical points, height
- Population in thousands
- Permanent lake, temporary lake, marsh
- Spring, well, reservoir
- Navigable canal; wharf, dock, lock
- Steep coast, fishing grounds, beach and dunes
- Sand and rocks covered at high tide
- Lights: fixed light, revolving light, flashing light
- Harbour light, light ship, semaphore, beacon buoy
- Depths: reef, shoal with depth marked
- Church, chapel, shrine
- Windmill, water-mill
- Quarry, mine
- Contours: With interpolated form lines
- Showing a basin or hollow
- Woods, Bushes and shrubs, Orchards, Gardens, Vines, Olives, Meadows

Symbols vary slightly from sheet to sheet in this series according to edition.

French 1:25 000 Map Series

N.P.7 ou N.31	Motorway
N.P.19 ou N.228	Trunk or National roads — 1st class
N.696	Trunk or National roads — 2nd class
D.P.5 ou D.12	Trunk or National roads — 3rd class
D.47	Département Roads — 1st class
D.38	Département Roads — 2nd class
	Département Roads — 3rd class
	Cobbled Surface — 1st class
	Cobbled Surface — 2nd class
	Works road
	Track way
	Footpath
	Roads on embankments
	Roads in cuttings
	Walled road
	Multiple track railway
	Single track railway
	Railway sidings
	State boundary
	Département, arrondissement boundaries
	Canton, commune boundaries
	Electricity transmission lines
	Bridges; stone, wood, iron, suspension, footbridge
	Dam with sluice, ford, ferry
	Stream, dried-up stream
	Canals, with lock, dock
	„ not navigable
	„ diversion, dried up
	Aqueducts, on the ground, on a viaduct
	Spring, fountain, well, cistern, water tower
	Reservoirs
	Lakes, permanent, temporary
	Shingle, gravel; marsh; peat bog
	Trigonometrical points
	Churches, bell tower, chapel, small chapel
	'Mairie', police station, monument, chimney
	Barracks, hospital, convent
	Important buildings, factory with chimney
	Camp, kiosk, market or warehouse
	Water-mill, windmill
	Gasometer, blast furnace, mineshaft, cave
	Walls, walls in ruins, ruins
	Cemeteries; Christian, Jewish
	Rocks, scree
	Quarry, sandpit
	Form lines
	Basin or hollow
	Hedge, hedge with trees
	Aerodrome
	Woods
	Coniferous woods
	Tall bushes or brushwood
	Low bushes or brushwood
	Gardens
	Orchards
	Nursery
	Poplars
	Vines
	Osiers

Swiss 1:50 000 Map Series

	Station
	Narrow gauge railway
	Chair lift
	Ski lift
	1st class road, over 5m. wide
	2nd class road, 3–5 m. wide
	3rd class road, 2 2–3 m. wide
	Minor road
	Unsurfaced track
	Footpath
	Glacier or snow track
	Ancient trackway
	Bridge
	National boundary with numbered boundary stones
	Canton boundary with boundary stones
	District boundary with boundary stones
	Parish boundary with boundary stones
△ 2042.6	Trigonometrical points
•1966.6 •1165.0	
•1482 •2364	Spot height
	House, house with drive, guest-house
	Church, chapel
	Gasometer, tower or high chimney, monument
	Ruin
	Walls, dry walls
	Monument, cross
	Cave, erratic boulder
	Marsh
	Rock and scree
	Landslide. Avalanche scar
	Glacier and moraine
	1 Thick woodland / 2 Open woodland / 3 Scrub
Over rocks / Over ice	Contours
	200 m interval
	20 m interval
	10 m interval
Hochdorf	Parish with 1000–5000 inhabitants
Seen	Village with 1000–5000 inhabitants
Kerns	Parish with less than 1000 inhabitants
Wasen	Village with 100–1000 inhabitants
Huben	Group of houses, 50–100 inhabitants
Eichmatt	Small group of houses

95

Linear Scales

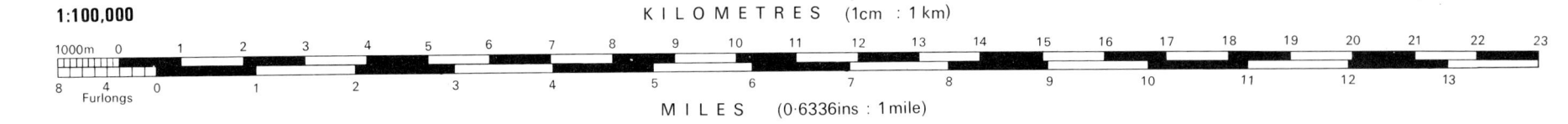

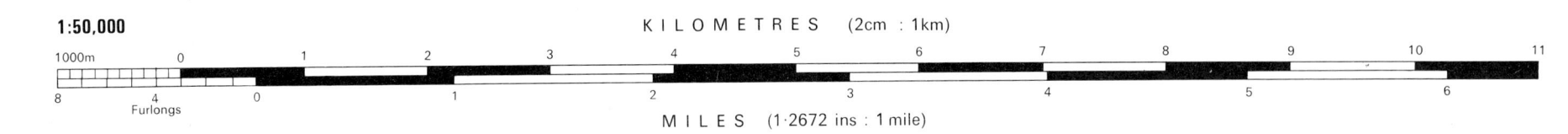

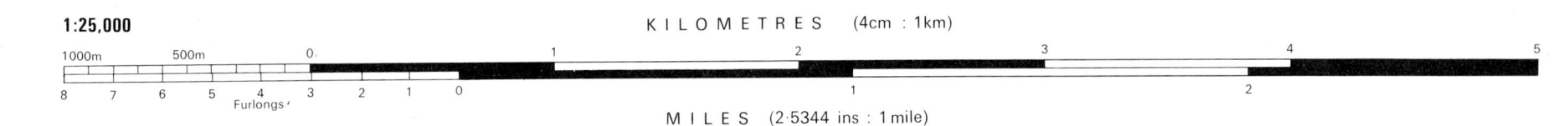

1:100,000   KILOMETRES (1cm : 1km)   MILES (0·6336 ins : 1 mile)

1:50,000   KILOMETRES (2cm : 1km)   MILES (1·2672 ins : 1 mile)

1:25,000   KILOMETRES (4cm : 1km)   MILES (2·5344 ins : 1 mile)

Tables for Conversion from Metric Measurements

Metres to Feet

Metres	Feet or Metres	Feet
0·305	1	3·281
0·610	2	6·562
0·914	3	9·842
1·219	4	13·123
1·524	5	16·404
1·829	6	19·685
2·134	7	22·966
2·438	8	26·247
2·743	9	29·528
3·048	10	32·808
7·620	25	82·022
15·242	50	164·043
30·480	100	328·086
76·200	250	820·220
152·420	500	1640·430
304·800	1000	3280·860

Kilometres to Miles

Kilometres	Miles or Kilometres	Miles
1·609	1	0·621
3·218	2	1·242
4·827	3	1·864
6·437	4	2·485
8·046	5	3·107
9·655	6	3·728
11·265	7	4·350
12·874	8	4·971
14·483	9	5·592
16·093	10	6·214
40·232	25	15·535
80·465	50	31·070
160·930	100	62·140
402·320	250	155·350
804·650	500	310·700
1609·300	1000	621·400

Hectares to Acres

Hectares	Acres
1	2·47
2	4·94
3	7·41
4	9·88
5	12·36
6	14·83
7	17·30
8	19·77
9	22·24
10	24·71
25	61·78
50	123·56
100	247·12

°Centigrade to °Fahrenheit

°Centigrade	°Fahrenheit
+25	+77
+20	+68
+15	+59
+10	+50
+ 5	+41
0	+32
− 5	+23
−10	+14
−15	+ 5
−20	− 4
−25	−13
−30	−22
−35	−31
−40	−40

To convert °C to °F
$$x\,°C = \frac{9}{5}x + 32 \;(°F)$$